The Complete Official Road Guide Of The Lincoln Highway

THE COMPLETE OFFICIAL
ROAD GUIDE *of*

THE
LINCOLN
HIGHWAY

Price One Dollar

Published by

THE LINCOLN HIGHWAY
ASSOCIATION

National Headquarters - Detroit, Michigan

A complete Index will be found on
page 161

Advertiser's Index page 166

TO THE MEMORY OF

Arthur R. Pardington

Late Vice-President and Secretary of The Lincoln Highway Association

THIS SECOND EDITION OF THE COMPLETE OFFICIAL ROAD GUIDE OF THE LINCOLN HIGHWAY ASSOCIATION IS RESPECTFULLY DEDICATED.

At the time of Mr. Pardington's death in 1915, Henry B. Joy, President of The Lincoln Highway Association said:

"In the death of A. R. Pardington, Vice-President of the Lincoln Highway Association, the patriotic work suffers an irreparable loss. His collaborators have lost a commanding officer of peerless efficiency, of unflagging effort even during failing health and physical distress, of unflinching judicial fairness, with a patriotic devotion to the cause of the great memorial, the Lincoln Highway, such as could not be exceeded in any cause.

Mr. Pardington's departure from among the directors and workers of the Association from one end of the Nation to the other will create a void which cannot be measured.

He gave of his own means and of himself so liberally that he stimulated every person with whom he came in contact to become a soldier in the cause of the Lincoln Memorial Way.

Stretched on his bed of suffering, knowing his approaching end, he gave his aides instructions verbally, as his waning strength would permit, so that the affairs of the Highway might go on after his departure in ways that he had thoughtfully planned.

His example of self-sacrificing devotion to the Highway has given the cause an ever-increasing army of followers who will aid more liberally by donations and personal work as the result of the Pardington example of devotion and patriotism.

No man ever had more loyal friends, and friends were worth more to him than the riches which he gave liberally to the work.

It is not too much to say, it is not enough to say, that the Lincoln Highway insignia stretching from Jersey City on the Hudson River to Oakland on the Pacific is more his work than that of any other man. Thousands have given dollars to the cause. Pardington gave himself."

Introduction

THE Complete Official Road Guide of the Lincoln Highway was issued first in 1915 in response to an insistent demand on the part of the ever increasing number of motorists who desired to make the transcontinental trip. The first edition contained many errors of more or less importance, the book having been produced under difficulties, due to causes beyond the control of the Association.

This second volume for 1916 is the result of three different transcontinental trips on the part of officers of the Association inspecting the Lincoln Highway's condition, and checking up carefully the information compiled in the 1915 guide. In this work the officers of the Association have been aided wonderfully by the hundreds of Lincoln Highway consuls or representatives located all along the route, and by others whose interest in the Highway has prompted them to supply information of interest and value to the tourist.

The difficulties of making a transcontinental drive have been immeasurably reduced during the past year through the co-operation of the people along the route and the communities through which the route passes. The distance has been cut down considerably by the elimination of curves and unnecessary detours from the line of directness, road improvement has gone on with increasing rapidity, and the accommodations have been at many points immeasurably improved.

The Lincoln Highway in the season of 1916 will be found to be marked for practically 100% of its distance, although in many places this marking is not as thorough as it should be. Nevertheless it is possible to find one's way across the country on the Lincoln Highway without the necessity of making inquiries.

A trip across the Lincoln Highway in 1916 should be, with fair weather, a tour of great interest and pleasure, in which the element of danger is completely lacking. Of course, disregard of the simple precautions necessary in undertaking any long tour in any part of the United States will mean inconvenience and discomfort. The suggestions given in the following pages for the equipment of both car and occupants for a transcontinental drive are made by veteran transcontinental tourists, and should be carefully considered by any one undertaking a cross-country trip for the first time.

National Headquarters

LINCOLN HIGHWAY ASSOCIATION.

March 30th, 1916.

President

The Lincoln Highway Tourist Follows an Historic Old Trail

By F. H. TREGO, Chief Engineer
The Lincoln Highway Association

BACK in the old frontier days there were seven trails crossing the great plains of the interior of the North American Continent.

None of these primitive highways, however, with the possible exception of the Old Santa Fe Trail, has a more stirring history of adventure and hardship than that known as the Salt Lake Trail; now the Lincoln Highway.

Over this route were made the historic expeditions of Fremont, Stansbury, Lander and others to the heart of the Rocky Mountains and beyond to the shores of the Pacific, and the lonely migrations of the Mormons to the valley of that vast inland sea, the Great Salt Lake, were also made on this same route. These same Mormons, by marvelous surmounting of almost insuperable difficulties and hardships turned the desert into one of the garden spots of the world.

Over this same trail through the western wastes, the Pony Express and the Overland Stage Coach made their dusty perilous way, ofttimes leaving a trail of bloodshed from battles with the Indians.

Buffalo Bill, that historic character of the plains, began his adventurous career as a boy on this trail, and laid the foundations of a life which has made his name well known to every schoolboy in the land.

Whereas, the original travelers over the Salt Lake Trail generally started at St. Louis, Missouri, and proceeded up the Missouri River to about the point where Kansas City is now situated,—or to where Atchison is now—the Lincoln Highway comes in from the east and crosses the Missouri River at Omaha, Nebraska. It then cuts across and strikes the Platte River in Lat. 41 deg. 20 min. north and Longitude 96 deg. 20 min. west, thereafter following the course of the Platte River to a point near Fort Kearney—now Kearney, Nebraska,—where it meets the Old Salt Lake Trail.

In the days of the "Forty Niners," the emigrants to far off California followed this old trail from Kansas City, and even today the many tracks of those heavy, ox drawn wagons may be seen, cut deeply into the soil of the plains along the Lincoln Highway.

One of the most pathetic accounts of these many adventurers is that of the Donner Party. Leaving their homes and farm lands in Illinois, full of hope for success in that land of promise, California, only to starve within a day's journey of their goal, buried in the bitter cold of the snow storms of the Sierra Nevada Mountains, where misfortune overtook them.

9

And this after braving six months of danger from Indians and the perils of the desert.

The trail follows the course of the North Platte River to a point near what is now Granger, Wyoming; then down the Big Sandy Creek to Old Fort Bridger. From there thru the beautiful Parley's Canyon into the valley of Salt Lake.

From Salt Lake, the Desert is crossed to Reno, Nevada, and then, after climbing the great Sierras, it passes Bear Valley and on into the fertile plains of the Sacramento River and to the Pacific Ocean and San Francisco.

As one speeds over the Lincoln Highway in his modern automobile, it is hard to realize the slow moving oxen, painfully dragging the cumbersome "prairie schooner" of '49, the women and children riding inside the canvas covered body, the stifling heat, the dust of the desert rising in choking clouds, the attacks by Indians, the want of water and sometimes food and all the suffering and yearning, with the births and deaths which must have occurred in that journey of six or seven months—an almost interminable journey which now is made from coast to coast in twenty days with nothing but enjoyment from one end to the other. Deserts which required weeks of weary travel with the energy of desperation are now passed in but a few hours.

The West may well be proud of such a people as braved the journey and survived to reach her fertile valleys, and the tourist should realize these things if the most is to be gained from a flying trip across these United States.

There are many wonderful things to see, as you pass along the Lincoln Highway, some historic, some scenic; but above all, the greatest impression which will be left with you, will be the immense size of this, our country. The thickly settled East, with its farms and frequent houses, the vast rolling prairies of the Middle West, where the buffalo used to roam in countless herds, the dreary deserts, the majestic mountains, and finally sweet California, wafting to you the odor of orange blossoms and roses with the breeze as you approach the Golden Gate.

New sensations and a few thrills await the dweller of the East when first he makes the transcontinental tour over the Lincoln Highway. New sensations are the spice of life and this country of ours is full of them to the lover of scenery, and many wonderful works of nature are open to him who will make just a little effort to see.

An uplifting of the soul is sure to follow this contact with Nature in her majesty, and Self becomes smaller and smaller as we realize the immensity of things in traversing this country. Pride in our country rises to heights unsuspected before the commencement of the journey.

To stand upon the great desert amidst overwhelming silence, gazing with awe at the glorious, yet delicate, coloring of the sky and distant mountains in the cool of the dawning day or in the fading light of evening, is worth all of the little hardships of the tour; and then to pass through the cool forests of the Sierras, on a fine road, with great fir trees on all sides, and roaring water tumbling over rocks alongside, makes us glad that we have lived to see and feel such things.

European countries fade beside the immense expanse of western America. There are many good roads thru wonderful places in the West, and each year a new route may be taken, each one being worth any hardship to the lover of travel.

The Pony Express

ON the third day of April, 1860, at noon, the Pony Express started from Sacramento—the western terminal—and from St. Joseph, Missouri—the eastern terminal. The run of 1966 miles was made in ten days and later the trip was repeatedly made in nine days

The big New York newspapers printed special editions on tissue paper for the Pony Express and all letters were written on the thinest paper obtainable. The mail matter was placed in leather saddle bags and sealed, and these bags were transferred from pony to pony about every ten miles all the way across.

The trail of 2,000 miles was infested with "road agents" and hostile savages who roamed in formidable bands, ready to murder and scalp any white person they were able to catch. The Express rider had to depend on his pistols, his wits and to the fleetness of his horse to elude these dangers.

Five hundred horses were required with 190 stations, 200 station keepers and 80 experienced riders.

The Overland Stage Coach

THE first starting point of the Overland Stage Line was at Leavenworth, on the Missouri River; but after a few months, it was changed to what is now Atchison.

The trip to Sacramento was often made in fifteen days, a distance of nineteen hundred miles. The United States Government paid this company $800,000 each year for the transportation of the mails. Twenty-five cents was charged for each letter.

The Indians frequently attacked the stage, killing the guards and passengers and running off the stock; generally burning the coach. Robbers also furnished their quota of troubles and sometimes obtained as high as $70,000 as a prize for their daring.

During the Civil War, the route was changed from South Pass to Bridger's Pass on the Cherokee Trail, following Fremont's survey of 1843 instead of the route through Fort Laramie; thus coinciding with the Lincoln Highway through this section of Wyoming.

11

Facts of Interest to Transcontinental Tourists

By H. C. OSTERMANN, Field Secretary
of The Lincoln Highway Association

Editor's Note: H. C. Ostermann, Field Secretary of the Lincoln Highway Association, has spent practically all of his time for the past three years on The Lincoln Highway between New York and San Francisco, and has possibly driven that route more times than any other man. He is therefore thoroughly familiar with conditions along the route, and his advice to the motorist about to undertake a transcontinental tour is the result of wide experience and can well be relied upon.

WHEN I first drove across the United States in a motor car in 1908 and again in 1912 there was no such thing as a transcontinental road. Few people had driven across the country, and the innumerable difficulties with which the motorist undertaking a transcontinental drive was forced to encounter made the trip possible only to those who enjoyed hardships and a rough outing, and who had the time to devote to a drive which might take sixty days or ninety, depending upon the conditions of the roads and the luck one had in finding good ones, and in getting across the different States in as direct a manner as possible. In those days one started out with no very clear conception of exactly what route would be followed and proceeded across the country in a more or less uncertain fashion, inquiring at different points the best road to follow to the next city west. It was impossible to estimate with any degree of accuracy the length of time to be required in reaching the coast, the cost of the trip, or in fact to foretell whether it would be possible to complete the journey at all or not.

Since the inception and announcement of the Lincoln Highway in 1913, it has been a wonderful experience to watch the growth and development of this transcontinental road. No one who has not practically spent the entire time from 1908 to the present date in driving back and forth across the country can have the slightest conception of the tremendous amount of work and effort which has been expended in bringing the Lincoln Highway to its present condition. It is true that there is a tremendous amount of work yet to be accomplished on the road, but nevertheless the work which has been done enables any man to plan a transcontinental trip, knowing exactly what route he will follow, exactly through what cities he will go, and to determine in advance an approximate schedule of arrival at the different points, and to estimate with an amazing degree of accuracy the length of time it will take him to complete his journey and what the expense of the trip will be.

In 1912 it is probable that there had been less than a dozen through transcontinental trips by motor car actually completed entirely under the car's own power. The development of the route is shown in the fact that conservative estimates place the number of motorists who made the transcontinental drive last year at between fifteen and twenty thousand from the Missisippi River to the Pacific coast. Instead of sixty days or more now being required to drive from the Atlantic to the Pacific, the ordinary, unhurried progress of a pleasure party can make the trip in less than thirty days, provided of course the weather conditions are favorable.

If we assume that the tourist encounters perfect weather entirely across the country, absolutely no difficulties may be considered. Practically the only difficulties at present attendant upon a transcontinental drive over the Lincoln Highway are the result of unfavorable weather conditions. This is due to the fact that so much of the road is yet natural dirt highway, and while kept in perfect condition by the constant endeavor of the local committees in dry weather, a season of unusual rainfall inevitably makes driving difficult. It is wise for the transcontinental motorist to take as a precept a statement that when it rains in the middle west or west, the thing to do is to stop and not attempt to continue the journey until the rainy spell is over, and the roads have had a day or two to dry up. It is possible, and in fact I have myself been able, to drive across the United States without encountering a single day of rain, but this naturally is not the usual or probable experience. You can drive anywhere between New York and the Indiana-Illinois line either during or after heavy rainstorms without difficulty, but once west of this point it is wise to delay the trip, as many days as necessary, stopping comfortably at a hotel, if heavy rainstorms are encountered. You will make more progress in the end, and you will be saved many disagreeable experiences. It is hard work and can be considered nothing less, driving across either Illinois, Iowa or Nebraska during or just following heavy rains. Yet the pleasure and beauty of a drive across these States in fair weather has been compared to a drive across southern France, and in dry weather the roads are comparable with those of France.

A journey from the Atlantic to the Pacific by motor car is still something of a sporting proposition. It differs from a tour of the Berkshire Hills or any of the popular, extensive drives in the northeastern part of the United States. Any such accommodations and roads as the eastern tourist is accustomed to must not be expected. You must cheerfully put up with some unpleasantness, as you would on a shooting trip into the Maine woods, for example. Yet there are no hardships nor experiences which make the trip one of undue severity, even to a woman. My wife has accompanied me on many of my transcontinental trips, and for one who, like her, enjoys an outing, the minor hardships and unpleasant situations which may occasionally be encountered are only a part of the adventure. Those who want luxury and ease on a transcontinental trip should take a de luxe train. To

14

those who love the wide open spaces of the great west, and who· enjoy exertion and the clear pure air of the western plains and the high altitudes of the Rockies and the Sierras, the trip is a delightful outing.

The only thing which might make a coast to coast automobile trip unduly arduous now would be lack of proper equipment or the forethought to provide those necessities which experience has shown should be taken on a trip across the west. The tourist should also make certain that he leaves his destination at the proper time of year, so that weather conditions will be most favorable during his entire journey.

Cost of the Trip

THE entire expense of a car and four passengers from New York to San Francisco, a distance of 3331 miles, via the Lincoln Highway, should not at any time exceed $5.00 a day per passenger. This sum will include everything except tire expense and unforseen accidents. In it I have included gasoline, oil and all provisions, but have not figured the repairs to the car caused by breakage or wear. The expense of the trip can be increased to any figure, of course, by making use of high priced hotels in the larger cities for extended periods.

The above estimate places no restrictions upon the amount or quality of provisions, and will easily cover the requirements of the average person, even allowing for five or six meals in hotels in such cities as Philadelphia, Pittsburgh, South Bend, Omaha, Cheyenne, Salt Lake City and Reno. Even a party which is camping out entirely across the country wants to stop at a hotel about this often.

The Time Required

IT is of course possible to lengthen out a transcontinental drive to any extent desired, depending on the number and length of the side trips taken, and the amount of time spent at different points of interest. The usual pleasure party, however, with easy driving and only a nominal amount of sight-seeing at the different points, can make the trip in twenty to thirty days, driving approximately ten hours per day. This estimate means that approximately 18 miles per hour must be made during the driving time as an average. It is possible of course for many long stretches to greatly exceed this speed. The wide open stretches of the west, where small traffic is encountered, enables the driver to make any speed of which the car is capable.

Quality First

3400 r. p. m. Chalmers Brings Gallant Going

The new 3400 r. p. m. Chalmers lends a new enchantment to the Lincoln Highway. The magic of 3400 r. p. m. adds many miles to the life of your tires and flavors motoring with rare and pungent pick-up. This car's supreme engine speed makes a gallon of gas repay you 18 miles of gala going.

5-Passenger Touring Car or 3-Passenger Roadster, $1050 Detroit; $1475 in Canada—3-Passenger Cabriolet, $1400 Detroit; $1900 in Canada. Colors: Meteor blue, or Oriford maroon with gold stripe.

Chalmers Motor Company,   -   Detroit, Michigan

Don'ts for Tourists

THERE are a few don'ts which every tourist should store away in his mind for future use. They will come in handy some time during the coast to coast trip.

Don't wait until your gasoline is almost gone before filling up. There might be a delay, or it might not be obtainable at the next point you figured on. Always fill your tank at every point gasoline can be secured, no matter how little you have used from your previous supply.

Don't allow your water can to be other than full of fresh water, and fill it whenever you get a chance. You might spring a leak in your radiator, or burst a water hose.

Don't allow the car to be without food of some sort at any time west of Salt Lake City. You might break down out in the desert, and have to wait some time until the next tourist comes along.

Don't buy oil in bulk when it can be avoided. Buy it in the one gallon original cartons.

Don't fail to have warm clothing in the outfit. The high altitudes are cold, and the dry air is penetrating.

Don't carry loaded firearms in the car. Nothing of this kind is in the least necessary except for sport, anyhow.

Don't fail to put out your camp fire when leaving.

Don't forget the yellow goggles. In driving west you face the sun all afternoon, and the glare of the western desert is hard on the eyes.

Don't forget the camphor ice. The dry air of the west will crack your lips and fingers without it.

Don't build a big fire for cooking. The smaller the better.

Don't ford water without first wading through it.

Don't drink alkali water. Serious cramps result.

Don't wear new shoes.

As a help to tourists making a coast to coast trip over the Lincoln Highway, and from a knowledge which has been dearly bought with experience, I offer a few suggestions and also a list of supplies which it has been found advisable to carry. These supplies largely depend upon the taste of the individual and the nature of the trip being made, but there are some things which should not be omitted from the outfit under any circumstances.

In case of a break down or delay, hunger or thirst are not pleasant companions, nor can a man work if his mouth is dry from dust and lack of water.

Camping directions will be useful when the party gets west of Omaha, Nebraska, the point where most people begin to camp, although it is not necessary to camp at all if you do not so desire.

No extra gasoline need be carried, although it is advisable to have an extra tank for use in case of emergency, such as a leak in your gas tank or a break in your gasoline connections.

Backed by
Prest-O-Lite
Service

The Beginning of the End of Your Battery Troubles

The Prest-O-Lite Storage Battery is unique from two standpoints.

First:—Because of the unlimited facilities back of its manufacture, a better storage battery cannot be produced, size for size. On thousands of cars, the Prest-O-Lite Storage Battery is proving its superiority over other existing types in capacity, voltage, maintenance, and freedom from internal heating.

Second:—Not only is it a better battery but is backed by expert, universal battery service, unequalled and unapproached. The Prest-O-Lite Company maintains more Direct Factory Branches and Service Stations than all other battery makers combined. These service stations form the nucleus for the largest amount of actual service obtainable in the storage battery field.

There is a Prest-O-Lite Battery of correct shape, size, voltage and capacity for every make and model of car, and for every starting and lighting system which is or ever has been in general use.

Ask any Prest-O-Lite Battery Dealer or Service Station for details.

ATLANTA
BALTIMORE
BOSTON
BUFFALO
CHICAGO
CINCINNATI
CLEVELAND
DALLAS
DAVENPORT
DENVER
DES MOINES
DETROIT
INDIANAPOLIS
JACKSONVILLE
KANSAS CITY
LOS ANGELES
MEMPHIS
MILWAUKEE
MINNEAPOLIS
NEW YORK
OMAHA
PHILADELPHIA
PITTSBURGH
ST. LOUIS
ST. PAUL
SAN ANTONIO
SAN FRANCISCO
SEATTLE
SYRACUSE

The Prest-O-Lite Co., Inc.

907 Speedway   -   Indianapolis, Ind.

Each of these factory Branches is fully equipped for Battery Repairs and Service.

Keep your tank filled as full as possible at all times. Fill it at each opportunity, no matter whether it is low or not. Then you will never be without it.

In sleeping on the ground, dig a trench or shallow indentation across the bed location for the hips. You will sleep much easier. Make it about one inch deep, with round edges about 8 inches wide, and the full width of the sleeping bag.

Put shoes, etc. under the edge of the sleeping bag, even in fair weather, as the dew is very heavy in the west. Several light blankets are warmer than one or two heavy ones. A cotton comfort with the blankets will keep out the wind.

The regular sleeping bag constructed for the purpose is the best thing to carry, if you intend to sleep out. These bags can be secured at any good sporting goods store, and will contain all the necessary blankets and quilts, with an outside waterproof covering.

Start early and stop before dark to select a camp site. If you wait until dark you may be unable to find a spot free from rocks.

Always camp on high ground—never by water on account of mosquitoes.

Car Equipment

1	Lincoln Highway Radiator Emblem.
1 pair	Lincoln Highway Pennants.
2 sets	Tire Chains.
6 extra	Cross Chains.
1	Sparton Horn.
1 set	Chain Tightener Springs.
1 set	Tools.
2	Jacks.
1 pair	Good Cutting Pliers.
2 extra	Tire Casings.
4 extra	Inner Tubes.
1	Casing Patch.
3	Spark Plugs.
8 feet	High Tension Cable.
8 feet	Low Tension Cable.
1 extra	Valve and Spring, complete.
3	Cans Oil, in one gallon cans.
1	Axe.
1	Shovel (medium size).
1	Upper Radiator Connection.
1	Lower Radiator Connection.
1 set	Lamp Bulbs.
1	Motometer.

Optional Camp Equipment

1	5 gal. Milk Can with stay straps (for water, west of Cheyenne, Wyoming).
1	Canteen, 2 quarts.
1	Frying Pan, 10 in.
1	Grate for camp fire, 12" x 24".
1	Coffee Pot, 2 quarts.
4	Cups, large.
4	Pans (deep) 5" diameter.

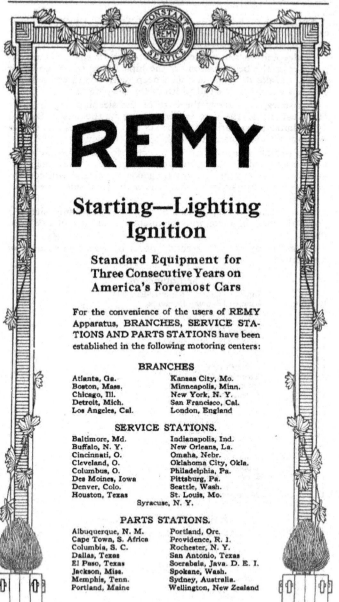

REMY

Starting—Lighting Ignition

Standard Equipment for Three Consecutive Years on America's Foremost Cars

For the convenience of the users of REMY Apparatus, BRANCHES, SERVICE STATIONS AND PARTS STATIONS have been established in the following motoring centers:

BRANCHES

Atlanta, Ga.	Kansas City, Mo.
Boston, Mass.	Minneapolis, Minn.
Chicago, Ill.	New York, N. Y.
Detroit, Mich.	San Francisco, Cal.
Los Angeles, Cal.	London, England

SERVICE STATIONS.

Baltimore, Md.	Indianapolis, Ind.
Buffalo, N. Y.	New Orleans, La.
Cincinnati, O.	Omaha, Nebr.
Cleveland, O.	Oklahoma City, Okla.
Columbus, O.	Philadelphia, Pa.
Des Moines, Iowa	Pittsburg, Pa.
Denver, Colo.	Seattle, Wash.
Houston, Texas	St. Louis, Mo.
	Syracuse, N. Y.

PARTS STATIONS.

Albuquerque, N. M.	Portland, Ore.
Cape Town, S. Africa	Providence, R. I.
Columbia, S. C.	Rochester, N. Y.
Dallas, Texas	San Antonio, Texas
El Paso, Texas	Soerabaia, Java. D. E. I.
Jackson, Miss.	Spokane, Wash.
Memphis, Tenn.	Sydney, Australia.
Portland, Maine	Wellington, New Zealand

20

4	Knives
6	Forks
6	Teaspoons.
2	Cooking Spoons.
4	Soup Spoons.
1	Dipper.
8	Plates, 8" diameter.
2	Stew Pots, (to nest)
1	Cooking Fork, 3 prong.
1	Carving Knife, butcher type.
3	Bars Ivory Soap.
6	Dish Towels.
1	Can opener
1	Bread Pan (for dish washing).
1	Bucket with lid.
1	Can for Pepper.
1	Patent Egg Carrier (1 dozen).
1	Cork Screw.
1	Air-tight Coffee Can 2 pound.
1	Air-tight Tea Can ½ pound.

Personal Equipment
Each Man

1	Lincoln Highway Association Membership Card.
1	Lincoln Highway Lapel Button.
1	Waterproof Sleeping Bag (warm type).
1	Waterproof Duffle Bag, 15 in. x 36 in.
	No suit case or satchel should be carried.
1	Pair Light Moccasins.
2 pair	Kahki (or Duxbac) Riding Trousers.
2	Army Officer's Shirts (best quality for warmth).
1 pair	Light Weight Shoes.
1 pair	Heavy Weight Shoes (loose enough for heavy socks.)
2 pair	Heavy Wool Socks.
2 suits	Heavy Wool Underwear.
2 suits	Light Linen or Cotton Underwear (to wear under the wool or alone—don't wear wool next to skin.)
2	Bandana Neck Kerchiefs.
6	Pocket Handkerchiefs.
3 pair	Medium Weight Socks.
1	Teamster's Canvas Coat, slicker and flannel, lined and with a high collar.
1 pair	Canvas Puttees.
1 stick	Camphor Ice.
2 dozen	Cathartic Tablets.
1 package	Gauze.
3 rolls	Gauze Bandages, 1½ in. wide.
1 tube	Vaseline (for guns and burns).
1	Tooth Brush.
1	Comb.
1	Knife (strong), two or three blades.
1	Pocket Compass.
1	Safety Razor.
1 can	Shaving Soap, Powder.
1	Shaving Brush.
1	Mirror (small).
	Needles and Thread.
1 package	Bachelor Buttons.
1 pair	Scissors (small).
2 pair	Gloves, gauntlet.
1	Belt, leather.
1	Inexpensive Open Face Watch.

1	Rubber Sheet, 6 ft. x 7 ft..
1 pair	Yellow Goggles.
1 pair	White Goggles.
1 sq. yd.	Mosquito Netting.
1	Camera.
1	Cap.
1	Can Tooth Paste.

Provisions

This list of provisions is of course optional, and is not at all necessary, as supplies can be obtained all along the route. It is wise, however, to have some food in the car west of Salt Lake City.

1	Slab Best Bacon.
3 cans	Peaches.
3 cans	Pineapple.
3 cans	Tomatoes.
3 cans	Baked Beans.
1 dozen	Eggs.
4 loaves	Bread.
1 sack	Salt.
1 can	Pepper.
1 pound	Butter (not necessary).
2 pounds	Rice.
10 pounds	Potatoes.
6 cans	Evaporated Milk (small size).
1 pound	Sugar.
1 package	Safety Matches (dozen boxes).
2 pounds	Cracked Wheat.
1 pint	Pickles.
1 box	Graham Crackers.
2 pounds	Coffee (ground).
½ pound	Tea.
1 roll	Surgeon's Plaster, 1 in. wide, 5 yards (for sealing cans, etc.)
3 cans	Corn.
	Fresh Fruit, often as possible.

REMEMBER: In Illinois, Iowa and Nebraska, after heavy rains, that if the tourist will remain over in the community in which he is stopping for five or ten hours, it will enable him to proceed in comfort, as the roads are well graded and dry very rapidly. Such a delay will, in the end, save time and will save your car, your tires and your temper, and make your trip more enjoyable.

FOR the benefit of the transcontinental tourist the following page is devoted to a blank which may be filled in, torn out and returned to the Lincoln Highway Association at Detroit, Mich., ordering a membership in the Association or any of the material sold by the Association for the benefit of tourists and the advancement of the work.

THE LINCOLN HIGHWAY ASSOCIATION
DETROIT, MICHIGAN

City--------------------------------------

--------------------------------191----
Date

Please send me C. O. D.:

Certificate of membership in Lincoln Highway Association, with radiator emblem and membership card, at $5.00 □   *Check Here*

Pair of pennants in 4 colors bearing insignia of Association, at $1.00 □

Large wall map in colors 60x42 in., at $1.00 □

" " " " " Mounted on muslin with rollers, $2.00 □

Proclamation of Route printed on parchment (31x42) and beautifully framed, at $5.00 □

Pocket Map in Colors, 25 Cents Each □

Complete official road guide of the Lincoln Highway containing tourist map, $1.00 □

Lincoln Way Lapel Button, 25 Cents Each □

Check what you wish and mail it TODAY

Name--
        Write Name Plainly

Address--

23

Hotel and Garage Rates

IT will be noted that in the present issue, hotel and garage rates are not given, as they were in the 1915 edition of this guide. The difficulty in getting accurately the rates of different hotels in so many cities, and the confusion which in some instances developed over changes in rates during the course of a year, has prompted us to omit detailed figures from this guide. It will be understood by the tourist that in all of the larger cities, hotel accommodations of the usual varying degrees of excellence and price can be secured, according to the desires of the tourist. In the smaller towns, as the tourist gets farther west, it will be understood that the accommodations are more restricted in excellence and comfort, consequently are proportionately lower in price.

It will be found by the tourist that the hotels and garages located along the Lincoln Highway are particularly good in their treatment of tourists, and that no excessive charges are made. It has also been found that the not uncommon practice in smaller towns of charging motorists an excessive rate or a rate beyond that paid by the local residents or ordinary transient, is very infrequently encountered on the Lincoln Highway, where the hotel keepers generally appreciate the fact that future business depends upon the volume and regard of the transcontinental tourists, and where generally the hotel men are in touch with the Association and are firm supporters of the work, doing everything possible to advance the comfort of the cross-country tourist.

Lost Packages

IN the event of your losing from your car a package, suitcase, piece of car equipment, etc., do not necessarily consider that it is lost beyond recovery. We suggest that the tourist refer to his guide book and write to the Consul of the Lincoln Highway in the town nearest to the point where he discovers his loss, describing the lost property, and asking the Consul to report that loss to the local newspaper or to have it posted in the local post office. Tourists should request that any package so found be forwarded to them at a given address by express, delivery charges collect.

If YOU find a package, take it to the nearest Consul; give him your name, address, etc. These little courtesies help.

General Information

BETWEEN New York, on the Atlantic Seaboard and San Francisco, on the Pacific Coast, the Lincoln Highway passes through the

Capitals of 5 States:
New Jersey, Wyoming, Utah, Nevada, California.

County Seats: (76)
New Jersey 5—Pennsylvania 11—Ohio 9—Indiana 5—Illinois 4—Iowa 10—Nebraska 12—Wyoming 5—Utah 3—Nevada 6—California 6.

Towns including County Seats and Capitals, 400.

Includes Cities, Towns, Villages, R. R. Stations, Ranches and Points or Land Marks enumerated in Guide.

New England Tourists

May reach the Lincoln Highway by either of the two routes herewith furnished.

Boston to New York:

Boston to Worcester	43.9 mi.
Worcester to Springfield	51.0 "
Springfield to Hartford	26.9 "
Hartford to New Haven	37.1 "
New Haven to New York	74.9 "
Total	233.8 mi.

Or by way of Albany, Syracuse, Rochester, Buffalo, Erie and Cleveland, connecting with the Lincoln Highway at Mansfield, Ohio.

Boston to Worcester	43.9 mi.
Worcester to Greenfield	63.7 "
Greenfield to Pittsburgh	56.8 "
Pittsburgh to Albany	36.7 "
Albany to Syracuse	144.7 "
Syracuse to Rochester	96.1 "
Rochester to Buffalo	75.9 "
Buffalo to Erie	89.6 "
Erie to Cleveland	101.0 "
Cleveland to Mansfield	81.2 "
Total	789.6 mi.

Publishers' Note—Blue Book Mileages.

As to Mileages

IT will be noted that the early log of the Lincoln Highway, issued in the Fall of 1913, as well as the 1915 edition of the Complete Official Road Guide of the Lincoln Highway, will show material differences as to mileages when compared with the present volume. Also that the tourist will encounter at many points on the route signs which were erected in 1913 and 1914, or even later, and which may contain mileages which do not agree with those given in this volume. These differences in mileage are due to the constant effort of the Association, the states, the counties and the people along the route in shortening the total distance between the two coasts.

The present volume is as near accurate as possible, and supersedes all previous logs. As the work continues, each year will see decided shortening, due to the elimination of curves and unnecessary detours, and the mileages between points and between the two coasts will therefore continue to change as the Lincoln Highway more nearly approaches that ideal toward which the people of the nation are striving, the shortest, direct, connecting, improved Highway between the two coasts.

The rapidity with which the work of straightening the Lincoln Highway has progressed will be shown by the comparison of the figures in the log of 1913 with the total mileage given herein. The 1913 log showed a total mileage of approximately 3389 miles between New York and San Francisco. The log of the complete official road guide of 1915 showed an approximate total of 3384 miles, while it will be noted that the total distance as indicated herein is 3331 miles.

Warning as to Fires

THE Chief Forester of the Department of the Interior urges all tourists to use great care in extinguishing all matches, cigar or cigarette ends. This pertains particularly to those who may be touring in mid-summer or during prolonged dry spells.

He urges that those tourists who may from time to time camp by the roadside, completely extinguish all fires that may have been kindled. He suggests that these fires be stamped out or that a bucket of water be used. Water will be found in abundance at those points which are likely to be chosen for camp sites.

The Indian Agents urge the co-operation of tourists in their duties by refraining from furnishing liquor in any form to these wards of the Government. This practice in some instances has made it necessary to exclude tourists from certain Reservations. This is most unfortunate as a visit to one of these "concentration camps" is sure to prove of interest to the eastern tourist.

State License Regulations

New York Exempt if home state grants reciprocal privileges.

New Jersey Exempt for period of 15 days in any one year, if home state grants reciprocal privileges. Same applies to drivers' licenses.

Pennsylvania Exempt for period that home state grants reciprocal privileges.

Ohio Exempt provided home state laws have been complied with.

Indiana Exempt if registered in home state and front and rear non-swinging plates are shown.

Illinois Exempt for 60 days if home state grants reciprocal privileges and home plates are properly displayed.

Iowa Exempt provided home state grants reciprocal privileges and home plates are properly displayed.

Nebraska Exempt if registered in home state.

Wyoming Exempt if registered in home state.

Utah Exempt if registered in home state.

Nevada Exempt for 30 days.

California Exempt if registered in home state.

Note: Be sure your car is properly equipped with your home state plates (one each front and rear.) Have them securely attached because of the hard usage and possible theft by souvenir hunters.

Lincoln Highway Maps

A COMPLETE detailed map of the Lincoln Highway and the main improved connecting roads will be found inside the back cover of this volume. The Lincoln Highway is indicated in red, and the main feeder roads in blue. Additional copies of this map, separate from this volume, can be obtained by sending 25c to the headquarters of the Lincoln Highway Association, Detroit, Michigan, or from any Lincoln Highway Consul.

For touring bureaus, offices, etc. this same map in three colors is issued in a size 60″ x 42″. On heavy paper this map is $1.00. Mounted on muslin and rollers $2.00. These can be secured from the National Headquarters by sending forward the correct amount.

Lincoln Highway "Seedling Miles"

AT many points along the route of the Lincoln Highway in Ohio, Indiana, Illinois and Nebraska the tourist's attention will be called to strips of standard concrete road surface called Lincoln Highway seedling miles. These stretches of hard-surfaced road are built in these various communities with cement donated by the Lincoln Highway Association. This is done with the idea of encouraging similar construction in the same and other localities along the route. It is a self-evident fact that the traveler, be he a motorist or teamster, is certain to appreciate the value of hard-surfaced roads after traveling a distance upon one of these hard-surfaced seedling miles, and then dropping off into the rough going and ordinary dirt roads. The wonderful increase in improvement noted on the Lincoln Highway can be more or less directly traced to the lesson which these seedling miles is teaching.

Tourists Indebted to Guide Advertisers

The funds of the Lincoln Highway Association are devoted to the furtherance of road improvement, and the policy of the Association does not allow expenditures along any lines other than those aimed directly at the rapid improvement of the route itself. Consequently this volume which is so necessary for transcontinental tourists on the Lincoln Highway carries sufficient advertising to cover the expense of its publication. Those who are conversant with the work of the Association will appreciate the wisdom of this policy. Funds contributed to the Association for road building purposes are not touched for such expenses as the production of maps and other road information, necessary as they are to the tourist. The motorist is therefore indebted to those advertisers, who, by taking space in this volume, have made its publication possible. The small price at which the book is sold to the tourist is but a fraction of the actual cost necessary to secure the detailed information provided herein, and the work of compilation and publication.

The Association vouches for the advertisers whose announcements appear in this volume, and recommends that transcontinental tourists extend their patronage so far as possible and thus reciprocate for the aid these advertisers have given the Association in producing this volume for the use of the tourist

The Lincoln Highway Tour In 1916

By AUSTIN F. BEMENT, Secretary of the
Lincoln Highway Association

EVERY American motorist has within him something of the feeling that prompted our pioneer forefathers to explore the new and the unknown. Consequently automobile touring ranks high as a pleasureable recreation today. Your true motorist likes to settle down behind the wheel, knowing that his motor is running smoothly, and head away over new roads amid new surroundings, away from every-day places and things that have grown hum-drum through constant association. But he does not want to take the risks and chances the pioneer did, nor should he. The man in the automobile wants a passable road through a country that offers something worth while to see as he goes, and at night a good bed and the assurance of wholesome food.

It has always been possible to satisfy these demands in a more or less restricted way. Relatively short tours of merit exist in almost every part of the country. But to drive one's own car clear across the United States from one ocean to the other, over mountains and deserts and far away from the comforts and assistance to be had in the city, has in the past been too much to be thought of; impossible and foolhardy.

That is the opinion that held practically up to the summer of 1915 when the progress of Lincoln Highway improvement brought about a great change. Because of that opinion the American motorist has previously gone to Europe for his touring or has limited it to some certain sections of the eastern part of the country. The roads in Europe were known to be good, the hotel accommodations even in the smallest towns were acceptable and there was much of historical interest and beauty to be seen.

It has been conservatively estimated that the thousands of Americans that have yearly poured over seas to Europe, there to enjoy the perfect roads, magnificent scenery and historical points of interest, have carried with them, never to return, a sum in excess of two hundred million dollars. The American tourist has been one of the best sources of revenue in many a small English or European town. Hundreds of Americans are familiar with Waterloo who have never seen Gettysburg. The beauty of the Scottish lochs is familiar to many who have never visited the northern lake regions of Michigan and Wisconsin. The Druid temples of England have proven a source of interest to thousands who do not even know that in our southwest are Aztec structures which were overgrown with the vegetation of centuries when the Parthenon was building.

These are no new remarks to the Amercian tourist. For years we have talked and argued "See America first," when the means

31

of really seeing those portions of America most worth while have been lacking. The Berkshires, Catskills, and White Mountains are an old story to our eastern motorists, yet west of the Mississippi lies a vast empire larger than the whole of Europe, which to them has remained a closed book. It required much to turn our tourist westward, to travel under the rough conditions and indifferent accommodations found along our western trails.

Three factors stood out prominently as the reasons for what may be called the western touring boom, which became so evident during the summer of 1915. They were, the war in Europe, the improvement of the Lincoln Highway, which while being far from the European tour in the matter of either road conditions or accommodations, has through tremendous effort become at least acceptable to those who enjoy an outing at times more or less rough, and lastly, the Panama-Pacific Exposition and the San Diego Exposition in California, which provided the goal for the western trip.

When the Lincoln Highway was announced to the country in the Fall of 1913, the daily press and national publications devoted to it a vast amount of educational publicity and have ever since. The seed of proper understanding of America's worth to herself through the intercommunication to result from the building of great national highways was sown. The great war now raging on the other side of the Atlantic cut off both the desire and the possibility to visit foreign shores, and the Fairs in California offered a happy solution to the difficulties of those who demanded some place—any place to go by automobile.

Consequently the Summer of 1915 saw an increase in transcontinental touring of between 300 and 600 per cent. An estimate of the number of cars which entered California, the western terminus of the Lincoln Highway, can be obtained from the statement of D. E. Watkins, Secretary of the California State Automobile Association. He says, "Conservatively estimated, I would say, fully 25,000 automobile parties have toured to California. During the month of July, 1915, over 4,000 were supplied with touring information by the Association."

To show that this increase is general let me add a few more instances that have come to the attention of the National Headquarters of the Lincoln Highway Association. The Journal at Reno, Nevada, did some careful investigating of this subject, and found that in round numbers, 5,500 automobiles passed through that city, which is on the Lincoln Highway.

Mr. H. C. Ostermann, Field Secretary of the Lincoln Highway Association, reports that 33 automobiles registered at one garage in Cheyenne on the day he stopped there.

La Porte, Indiana, reports 35,000 "foreign" automobiles through that city on the Lincoln Highway. Pennsylvania has no figures that can be quoted, but the press agree that the increase in through touring was very large.

Here we have thousands and thousands of tourists who have seen their own country for the first time. It is beyond my power to describe the beauties and wonders that have passed before their eyes, but it is but fair to think that they will be apostles to the cause that furnished them their season's recreation, and that word of what they have enjoyed has been carried to the thousands more who have yet to respond to the spirit of "See America First," now for the first time becoming practical.

The first voicing of their tribute to their home land is now being sounded. Let me quote Mr. Charles Steckler, attorney, of New York City, who says, "Europe has nothing better than the scenery in this country. Even in the matter of climate Europe has nothing to compare with the United States. The great variety of scenery along the Lincoln Highway is a constant source of pleasure and interest to the tourist. This scenery is so different from anything found in Europe that it makes a wonderful impression on the motorist. In Europe everything is old, the towns and villages are old, the people and their customs are old, while in this country everything is new.

"The greatest variety of scenery is along the Lincoln Highway. It is the finest I have ever seen and is well worth a trip across the continent. The only way to see such scenery thoroughly is by automobile. It is impossible to get a thorough idea of the country in which we live without traveling over it in a motor car."

Officers of the Lincoln Highway Association completed last season a trip from New York to San Francisco, taking moving pictures all along the route of the great thoroughfare for exhibition throughout the country during the past Winter. There were four automobiles in their caravan, and the trip was made without a particle of mechanical trouble to any one of them. They report that they were at no time more than 50 miles from a source from whence all supplies for their cars might be obtained. No necessity existed for burdening themselves with extra weight. Everything needed could be purchased along the Way at a reasonable price.

A drive over the Lincoln Highway from New York to San Francisco is a wonderful exposition of what can be accomplished by organization, co-operation and concentration. Two years ago the route of the great memorial thoroughfare as an entity was unknown, the series of roads now forming it were unimproved, unmarked and in many places for long sections impassable. To drive across the continent then was a feat. Today the transcontinental driver is amazed at the amount of constructive work going on, not in certain states or counties but for mile after mile and day after day until he loses all track of its extent or location. The drive today is still a sporting proposition but nevertheless a common experience.

With the incorporation of the Lincoln Highway Association in the Fall of 1913, a central organization and clearing house for

33

effort were placed at the disposal of the many interests which individually were striving for results in their separate localities with small success. The Lincoln Highway crystallized national endeavor. A vast amount of careful work was expended in choosing a definite, logical transcontinental route; a proclamation of this choice, the great purpose of the Lincoln Highway as a tangible reality were placed before the people of the country in an appeal that reached the entire reading public.

Following this educational campaign conducted during the first year after the incorporation of the Association, material constructive results have followed one another so rapidly that but few realize the wonderful progress in actual building the Highway has enjoyed. Only one who attempted to drive across the country two years ago and who drives the same route this summer can appreciate this progress—it has been tremendous.

A few instances in point are of decided interest. The Lincoln Highway across New Jersey is entirely hard-surfaced and every mile is marked. Pennsylvania has spent $510,000 on the Highway in the past 18 months, and has but 18 miles that are dirt road. Ohio has spent over $700,000, bonded for $610,000 more and has 4 out of every 5 miles of the Way either concrete or brick. Indiana has built or bonded for 68 miles of hard-surfaced Lincoln Highway and is building the best type of road that money will buy. Illinois has gravel roads and is building seedling miles with the cement offered by the Lincoln Highway Association. Iowa has spent $250,000 in round figures and keeps her section graded, crowned, drained and dragged in the best possible manner. In dry weather there is no finer road on earth than the Lincoln Highway in Iowa. Nebraska has 5 sections of concrete construction now under way or completed. Wyoming, Utah and Nevada have no hard-surfaced roads, nor can they be expected there where the long mileage through a sparsely popluated country would make the cost prohibitive. But the spirit is there and all that can be done to aid the tourist is done by the individual ranchers along the route, as well as the state and county officials. California's part of the Highway needs no mention; her highways stand as an example to the whole nation.

The Lincoln Highway follows the path of the nation's progress as it expanded Westward. Its course holds closely to the old trails made famous in the East by the passage of Colonial and British, Federal and Confederate troops, and in the West by the early settlers and Indian fighters, the "pony express," the 49ers and all the vanguard of civilization who braved a thousand dangers in breaking the way.

Almost immediately upon leaving New York interesting historic points are passed. The Delaware is crossed not far from where Washington embarked his tattered host on their perilous course amid the floating blocks of ice. The Lincoln Highway traveler across Pennsylvania turns the pages of the nation's most thrilling history. In Paoli, near Philadelphia, the road runs but

34

a step from Valley Forge, where the Colonial troops spent the awful winter of 1778.

In Ohio, once the old frontier, scenes of Indian fights and massacres abound. Journeying onward across Indiana, Illinios, Iowa, Nebraska, Wyoming, Utah, Nevada and California, the traveler will continue to turn those thrilling pages of our nation's history; the history of her progress, her development, her achievement.

And to delight the eye wonderful ·treats for the lovers of nature's most alluring masterpieces are to be found. The wonders and beauty of the scenery along this 3331-mile transcontinental drive are unsurpassed by any to be found in any part of the globe. The variety of grandeur and charm of natural scenic splendor is past all description. The Lincoln Highway crosses the beautiful Appalachian Mountains, then onward across the gentle rolling farm lands of the middle west, the richest and finest in all the world. It crosses the space-bound plains of Nebraska and Wyoming, across the Rockies, and winds through the heights of the mighty Sierras, entering California by way of Lake Tahoe, "The Garden Spot of the Universe."

Here we have some idea of the Lincoln Highway as it exists today and offers to the American motorist the avenue to the enjoyment of his own country which has, up to the very recent past, been denied him.

The Eastern tourist driving the Lincoln Highway in 1916 must remember the difficulties which confront the western states in their efforts to present acceptable driving conditions on their main thoroughfares of travel. Many motorists across our great West content themselves with abusing the communities or the states when poor or even worse road conditions are encountered, as they often are, without giving a thought to the almost insurmountable obstacles with which those communities or states are confronted. Many a western county embraces a territory as large as some of our eastern states and contains a population of a few scattered thousands. If the Eastern tourists wants good touring conditions in the west his help must be had—everyone must do their part toward the rapid improvement of these sections of the Lincoln Highway which by no possibility and by no matter how great an effort can be improved without outside aid. The Lincoln Highway Association is a clearing house for the combined national effort which will some day result in our first great national road across the United States. Its problems are many and its work enormous. If you encounter a mud hole this summer in some western state—don't simply "kick"—help! Send in to the National Headquarters of the Lincoln Highway Association your share of that great fund which must be provided before a thorough connecting hard-surfaced, permanent route of travel can be established across the country. If only every motorist who drives the Lincoln Highway this season would aid the Association to the extent of but five dollars, many of the worst stretches could be permanently improved.

The Proclamation of the Route of
The Lincoln Highway
Issued September 10, 1913

WHEREAS, the purpose of this Association is to immediately promote and procure the establishment of a continuous improved highway from the Atlantic to the Pacific, open to lawful traffic of all descriptions and without toll charges, and

WHEREAS, toward the end of accomplishing this purpose elaborate research and investigation has been prerequisite to crystalization of opinion before intelligent and wise decision could be reached, and

WHEREAS, this Association expressly desires to impress upon all the people that it fully acknowledges that a public declaration by it of a route is of no force or effect except as it shall be wise and practical, and being so, meet with the approval of the people for such a useful and enduring memorial, and

WHEREAS, it is obvious that this Association can only aid and co-operate toward the desired end, and that UPON ALL THE PEOPLE, and especially upon the officials of each State and County and upon the inhabitants thereof, within the borders of which is designated by these resolutions a section of the Lincoln Highway does rest the patriotic burden of ESTABLISHING, BROADENING, STRAIGHTENING, MAINTAINING, AND BEAUTI-FYING such Highway to the end that it may become an appropriate memorial to the Great Martyred Patriot whose name it bears, and

WHEREAS, our chief step toward the desired goal is to crystalize in the public mind the practical wisdom of the route selected, therefore be it recorded here:

First—That in general it has been for nearly a century and is today the main Overland Trail, and that part lying West of Chicago is known by that historic name.

Second—It is the most direct and most practical route as to grades, curves and general topography.

Third—It is to the greatest extent improved and marked throughout it length.

Fourth—It is capable of being established as a fitting memorial highway at the least cost, and

WHEREAS, it is now proper to declare the results of deliberation and inspection in the hope that the wisdom and care in selection may insure united sentiment, and with the prayer that this record will appeal to the hearts of all patriotic Americans to the end that plans and activities toward construction may go immediately forward, therefore be it

RESOLVED, that the Lincoln Highway now is and henceforth shall be an existing memorial in tribute to the immortal Abraham Lincoln.

The Appeal to Patriots
Issued September 10th
1913

WITH the authority to plan and the power to execute of the great Napoleon, the Lincoln Way might be creditably planned and executed with dispatch from the beginning.

The idealists who have energetically pressed forward the great project of a Lincoln Highway from coast to coast have accomplished wonders towards crystalizing a nation-wide demand for the consummation of such a great and desirable project.

A committee of these idealists, after energetically and at their own personal expense pressing the propaganda to national fame and interest, decided to increase the force behind their efforts, enlist the financial aid of others, and thus develop a stronger public interest and support of the work.

After much deliberation they decided to centralize and organize with headquarters at a convenient center.

Route investigations began. All data was studied. Climatic conditions considered. Routes possible and impossible were traveled and details carefully noted as bearing on the ultimate decision which the Lincoln Highway Association was organized to make, as to what route would in its judgment be the most practicable to become the great Lincoln Memorial Highway.

The Lincoln Way so selected, if done wisely, will become great.

None know better than those who will assume to select the route that it is not done with Napoleonic authority or power.

The force behind the decision will be only the wisdom of it, which it is hoped will give the selection of route the force, because it is believed that the route of the "Lincoln Way," wisely chosen, will have behind it the patriotic force of the whole people.

The appeals of sections have been heard. The arguments of all interests have been and are being weighed.

Shall the Lincoln Way be marked on the map from large city to city? Shall it be from point of interest to point of interest?

Shall it be a highway from New York to San Francisco, as direct as practicable considering the limitations by Nature in the topography of the country?

See America first!

With all our force we endorse that sentiment! But a trans-continental highway that wound from large city to large city, from one wonder of nature to another would indeed be a devious and winding journey in this great America of ours.

It becomes plain that the decision on such a complicated route could not be arrived at in generations. No concentrated effort could be gained for the execution of the work. It becomes plain that the scope of the work must be within the practicable. It must be such as to immediately upon presentation gain your support and mine.

The decision must be confined to one permanent road across the country to be constructed *first*, no matter how desirable others may be and actually are.

Such has become the basic principle guiding the Lincoln Highway Association.

Pertinent Facts About the Lincoln Highway

THE Lincoln Highway is a continuous, connecting, improved road from the Atlantic to the Pacific, connecting New York and San Francisco, a distance of 3331 miles. The route is about one hundred and fifty miles longer than the shortest connecting transcontinental railroads, and is thirty-eight miles shorter than the transcontinental long distance telephone line.

The Lincoln Highway is being established by the Lincoln Highway Association, a patriotic and non-commercial body, incorporated under the laws of the State of Michigan, with headquarters in the city of Detroit.

The Lincoln Highway Association is not a constructing organization, but is a national body concentrating its attention upon the education of the public toward the proper expenditure of road funds in the securing of our first main arterial highway between the two coasts, a road which will be the first step in a national system of such permanent connecting routes.

The Lincoln Highway is open to lawful traffic of all descriptions without toll charges. At present the tourist encounters tolls in certain parts of Pennsylvania, but these will be removed as soon as certain legislation now pending is passed. Since the announcement of the route in 1913 many sections of toll road on the Lincoln Highway in Pennsylvania have been made public thoroughfares, and the work of eliminating these toll sections is going rapidly forward. Except at these points in the State of Pennsylvania and at bridges such as the one over the Mississippi River at Clinton, Iowa, nothing in the nature of toll charges is encountered. There is a nominal vehicle charge both in crossing the Hudson River and San Francisco Bay.

The basic principle followed in the laying out of the Lincoln Highway was to secure the shortest and most direct route between New York City and San Francisco, consistent with the topography of the country and serving the greatest possible proportion of the population. The Lincoln Highway serves 60 per cent of the population of the United States, and is directly available to 67 per cent of the registered automobiles.

Many pleasant trips to points of scenic and historic interest may be taken over the improved roads connecting with the Lincoln Highway. The Lincoln Highway passes only 18 miles south of Chicago, and tourists can easily and quickly reach the heart of the city over any of a number of improved roads.

The Lincoln Highway Association is promoting the construction of permanent hard-surfaced roads through a plan of "seedling mile" construction, by which the Association, through the co-operation of the cement companies of the United States, supplies counties with sufficient cement to construct a mile of concrete road of standard specifications. This plan has already resulted in the construction of the first two hard surfaced miles of road in the State of Nebraska, one near Grand Island and the other at Kearney. Other seedling miles have been placed in Illinois, near DeKalb and near Morrison, and plans for further seedling mile construction in 1916 in the States of Ohio, Indiana, Illinois and Iowa will be carried out. In every instance where seedling miles have been established through the co-operation of the Association with the local communities, the plan has resulted in an increase in the good roads sentiment of the county, and of that section of the state in which the construction was undertaken, and in further construction of like nature, either on the Lincoln Highway or on the main connecting roads.

The Lincoln Highway is now marked for the guidance of the tourist for its entire length, the general plan of marking being from five to eight standard markers to the mile, and two at the turns. All of this ideal system is not thoroughly completed. The sections of the route which are not thoroughly marked are mainly across the plains of the great west where the Lincoln Highway is the only road, and it is impossible for the tourist to go wrong. In these sections many times there will only be a marker at wide intervals of from five to ten miles, but enough to reassure the tourist that he is on the right road. The Association plans a thorough re-marking of the route in 1916 in a standard fashion from coast to coast.

Thousands of motorists have made the trip across the continent on the Lincoln Highway, and estimates vary from 5,000 to 20,000 cars crossing the counry from east of the Mississippi River to the Pacific coast by this route during the season of 1916. The Association estimates about 5,000.

The Lincoln Highway is by no means a good road for its entire distance, and in fact at many points the condition of the road depends entirely on the weather, and in wet weather will be found in very bad shape. The Association is striving in every way possible to remedy these conditions, and it is the poor condition of many sections of the route at present which makes necessary such an organization as the Lincoln Highway Association.

The task of completing, in hard surfaced material, a transcontinental road is one of tremendous difficulties and great cost, and while it will doubtless be many years before anything approaching the ideal toward which the Association is aiming will be accomplished, nevertheless tremendous strides are being made toward this ideal with every passing year, and the tourist who is properly prepared for the journey can at present make the trip a delightful outing, and if favored by weather conditions, complete the entire journey from one coast to the other in a month's time.

Officers and Directors
of
The Lincoln Highway Association

HENRY B. JOY, President,
    President Packard Motor Car Company,
    Detroit, Michigan.

CARL G. FISHER, Vice-President,
    President Prest-O-Lite Co.,
    Indianapolis, Indiana.

ROY D. CHAPIN, Vice-President,
    President Hudson Motor Car Co.,
    Detroit, Michigan.

AUSTIN F. BEMENT, Secretary,
    Detroit, Michigan.

H. C. OSTERMAN, Field Secretary,
    Detroit, Michigan.

EMERY W. CLARK, Treasurer,
    President First & Old Detroit Nat'l Bank,
    Detroit, Michigan.

W. F. COAN, Honorary Vice-President,
    Clinton, Iowa.

F. A. SEIBERLING,
    President Goodyear Tire & Rubber Co.,
    Akron, Ohio.

RUSSELL A. ALGER,
    Alger, Smith & Co.,
    Detroit, Michigan.

HON. ALBERT J. BEVERIDGE,
    Indianapolis, Indiana.

A. Y. GOWEN,
    Vice-President Lehigh Portland Cement Co.,
    Chicago, Illinois.

PAUL H. DEMING,
    The George Worthington Co.,
    Cleveland, Ohio.
    Vice-President American State Bank,
    Detroit, Michigan.

JOHN N. WILLYS,
    President Willys-Overland Co.,
    Toledo, Ohio.

New York

NEW YORK

N.Y.	S.F.	
0	3331	Pop. estimated to be about 5,333,000. The center of a population district of about 9,000,000. Times Square, Broadway and 42nd Street, the eastern terminus of the Lincoln Highway. To enumerate the accommodations for tourists in the way of hotels, garages, etc., would seem superfluous. The individual tastes and pocketbooks of all visitors to New York may be accommodated. If you are visiting New York for the first time, it is suggested that you provide yourself with the Tourist Guide of New York, and, if possible, join one of the parties and make a cruise around the water front of New York on one of the yachts regularly engaged in that service. Among the
	8	points of historic interest in New York City well worth the attention of tourists are the following: The City Hall; Battery Park; Castle Garden; The Old Block House, a relic of Revolutionary days, located in the northern extremity of the park, facing 110th Street; Fraunce's Tavern, a relic of Revolutionary days, and many other points which you will find enumerated in the New York City Guide. The terminus of the Lincoln Highway is in the immediate center of the theatre and hotel district of New York. Broadway and 42nd Street is said to be one of the most congested thoroughfare points in the city. Practically all of the hotels, you will find, maintain bureaus for the furnishing of information to transient visitors.

Leave Times Square (Broadway and 42nd St.) and proceed over West 42nd St. to Ferry.

New Jersey

L. H. STATE CONSUL, HORACE E. FINE,
Trenton, N. J.

GENERAL INFORMATION

NEW JERSEY, the "Golden State," was one of the original thirteen states and adopted the Federal Constitution in 1787. Historians and scientists of international reputation claim that man resided within the limits of this state at the close of the Age of Ice.

The native Indians, at the time of the settlement by the whites in the 17th century, were the Lenni Lenape; afterwards known as the Delawares.

This section of America was discovered and claimed by Holland

The entire course of the Lincoln Highway through New Jersey is hard-surfaced. Various types of paving are to be found in cities, and villages, while macadam prevails between. The entire route is carefully marked, and $60,000 in round figures have been spent in keeping the Lincoln Highway in shape during the last year.

A state law regulates speed in any part of New Jersey. It allows motorists to drive 25 miles per hour where houses are 100 feet apart, and 12 miles per hour where they are closer

New Jersey

together. Traffic regulations in any city or town are also controlled by state legislation, and are uniform.

JERSEY CITY

N.Y. S.F.
8   3323

5

Pop. 293,921. County seat, Hudson County. On the west bank of the Hudson River, at its entrance into New York Bay. Opposite to and connected with New York by various ferries and tunnels. Hotels and garages. Eight railroads, 3 express companies, 2 telephone companies. Extensive foreign and domestic commerce, iron, coal, produce and general merchandise. Several lines of European steamers have their docks here. Manufactories are numerous and varied including large locomotive and railroad supply houses, steel foundries and machine works, crucible and soap factories, grain elevators and sugar refineries which are among the largest in the world.

In 1812 the first steam ferry boat, designed by Robert Fulton, was put in operation between Jersey City and New York.

NEWARK

N.Y. S.F.
13   3318

5

Pop. 389,106. County seat, Essex County. On the Passaic River, which empties into Newark Bay three miles below the city proper.

Six hotels, rates from $1.00 up. Garages and automobile supply houses. Route marked through city and county, signs at city limits. Five railroads, 2 express companies, 2 telephone companies, broad and well paved streets, public parks, $350,000 library. Important trade and manu-

New Jersey

facturing center, having over $50,000,000 invested in its industries.

The celebrated Lincoln statute, by Gutzon Borglum, is located in front of the county courthouse, and is well worth a visit. Newark is the center of a population estimated to be about 1,000,000. L. H. Consuls, Joseph H. Wood, R. C. Jenkinson.

ELIZABETH

N.Y. **S.F.** Pop. 82,411. Alt. 33 feet. County seat, Union County.
18 **3313** Two hotels, rates $1.00 and $2.00, European. Twelve garages. Route marked through city and county. One railroad crossing at grade, protected. Six banks, 4 railroads, more than 2,000 stores, factories, etc., 2 express companies, 2 telephone companies, 2 newspapers, 14 pub-
5 lic schools, public buildings and parks. Commercial Club. L. H. Local Consul, Alex. J. Coleman.
Elizabeth was the first English settlement in this state, being purchased from the Indians in 1664, by settlers from Long Island.

RAHWAY

N.Y. **S.F.** Pop. 10,000. Alt. 22 feet. Union County.
23 **3308** One large hotel and several small ones. Six garages. Route marked through city and county. Two banks, Pennsylvania Railroad, 1 express company, 1 telephone company, 1 newspaper, 5 public schools, electric lights,
4 trolley and water works, Commercial Club.
The first dwellings were built about 1720. General Lafayette was entertained here on his visit to the United States in 1824.

ISELIN

N.Y. **S.F.** Pop. 220. Alt. 56 feet. Middlesex County.
27 **3304** Route marked through town and county. One railroad crossing at grade, protected. Two hotels, 1 railroad, 2 general business places, 1 express company, 2 telephone
1 companies, 1 newspaper, 3 public schools, electric lights. Commercial Club.

MENLO PARK

N.Y. **S.F.** Pop. 231. Middlesex County.
28 **3303** Railroad station, 1 express company. Menlo Park was the home of the first Edison laboratory and experimental
2 works. Here Edison invented the incandescent lamp and other of his great inventions.

METUCHEN

N.Y. **S.F.** Pop. 2692. Alt. 98 feet. Middlesex County.
30 **3301** One hotel, 2 garages. Route marked through city and county. One railroad crossing at grade, protected. One bank, 2 railroads, 2 express companies, 2 telephone com-
7 panies, 1 newspaper, 2 public schools, electric lights, trolley and water works. Automobile Club.

NEW BRUNSWICK

N.Y. **S.F.** Pop. 30,074. Alt. 120 feet. Middlesex County. On the
37 **3294** Raritan River.
Four hotels, rates $1.00 up. Twelve garages, 5 banks, 2 railroads, water connection to New York and Philadelphia,
1 approximately 250 general business places, 2 express companies, 2 telephone companies, 2 newspapers, 13 schools,

New Jersey

4 parks. Board of Trade, Automobile Club, Motorcycle Club. New Brunswick is the home of Rutgers College, chartered by George III in 1766, being then named Queen's College, also Dutch Reform Theological Seminary.

HIGHLAND PARK

N.Y. **S.F.** Pop. 2901. Middlesex County.

38 **3293** Suburb of New Brunswick.

5

FRANKLIN PARK

N.Y. **S.F.** Pop. 540. Alt. 133 feet. Middlesex County.

43 **3288** Route marked through town and county. One public school.

6

KINGSTON

N.Y. **S.F.** Pop. 400. Alt. 60 feet. Somerset County.

49 **3282** Two hotels, 1 garage. Route marked through town and county, signs at town limits. One railroad crossing at grade, protected. One railroad, 9 general business places, 1 express company, 1 telephone company, 1 public school, electric lights.

3 It was at this point that Washington with the American troops deceived the British on the day of the battle of Princeton, by filing off to the left at the church down the narrow road leading to Rocky Hill.

New Jersey

PRINCETON

N.Y. **S.F.** Pop. 5,136. Alt. 217 feet. Mercer County.
52 **3279** Four hotels, 4 garages. Route marked through city and county, signs at city limits. Three banks, 1 railroad, 1 express company, 3 telephone companies, 3 newspapers, 3 public schools, electric lights, trolley and water works.

5 Princeton University, 1,599 students; (founded 1746). Home and burial place of the late President Grover Cleveland. For years the home of President Wilson, who was President of the University. Carnegie Lake, the largest artificial lake in the world, donated by Andrew Carnegie.

LAWRENCEVILLE

N.Y. **S.F.** Pop. 207. Alt. 123 feet. Mercer County.
57 **3274** One hotel, 2 garages, 2 railroads, 10 general business places, 2 express companies, 1 telephone company, 1 newspaper, 3 public schools, electric lights, trolley and water works.
6 Lawrenceville Academy is one of the most famous schools for boys in the United States.

TRENTON

N.Y. **S.F.** Pop. 106,831. Alt. 33 feet. State Capital. County seat,
63 **3268** Mercer County. On the Delaware River. Leading manufacturing city.

Ten hotels, rates $1.00 up. 16 garages. Route marked through city and county. Two railroad crossings at grade, protected. Toll bridge over Delaware River, 10c-40c. Seven banks, 2 railroads, several hundred business places, 2 express companies, 2 telephone companies, 9 newspapers, 36 public schools, public buildings and parks, paved streets, electric lights, 3 trolley lines and water works. Extensive factories, wire mills, potteries, rubber mills, brass goods, candy manufacturers, etc. Numerous educational institu-

7 tions in vicinity. Home of New Jersey State Consul Horace E. Fine.

Before 1664 Dutch and Swedish peltry hunters came to Trenton to trade with the Indians. The Society of Friends (Quakers) was formed here in 1677.

In 1758 barracks for the King's troops were erected here on account of the French and Indian wars, and some of the buildings are still preserved.

On December 26th, 1776, Washington crossed the Delaware River with his little army and surprised the Hessians under Rall while they were still drunk from celebrating Christmas night. He made the passage through the ice floes with 2400 men and 18 cannon.

Intermediate Mileages

THE difficulty of accurately checking intermediate mileages between cities or points on the Lincoln Highway with the mileages indicated in this volume will be appreciated. This of course is due to the difference existing in the size of wheels, speedometers used, character of the road surface and other such considerations, but the main difference will be due to control points.

Wherever a natural control point exists, such as the city square or prominent public building in the center of a town, the mileages in this guide have been figured from that point to the next like control. In other instances the mileage is figured from town limits to town limits.

The figure in the open margin between the names of each two points on the Lincoln Highway indicates this intermediate mileage, and is only approximate, due to the reasons given above. This mileage will serve the purpose of the tourist, however, in indicating very closely the distance from each point to the next, and can be used in judging the extent of a day's trip or in laying out the schedule of a transcontinental journey.

A tourist driving into a small community where accommodations are limited, early in the evening can, by referring to these intermediate mileages and to the character of road surface indicated in the text, determine whether it would be wise to continue on to the next town, where possibly better accommodations for the night may be secured. These mileages are given for this reason and for the laying out of daily schedules, and are not intended to check closely with the speedometer of the tourist. It would be impractical to give fractional mileages in detail over such a long journey as is comprised between the two coasts. No two speedometers would check over such a distance, and without frequent predetermined control stations these mileages would be of no value.

The Lincoln Highway Association is planning on the establishment of definite control stations at each point on the Lincoln Highway, and it is expected that during the present year a great many such stations can be determined upon and the point marked with a distinctive sign bearing the Lincoln Highway marker and the words "control station." Minor conveniences of this kind for the tourist are being taken up by the Association as rapidly as possible. With the co-operation of the communities along the route it is hoped that definite control points can be located and marked for a very considerable portion of the route before the opening of the touring season of 1917.

Pennsylvania

GENERAL INFORMATION

THE tourist crosses the Delaware River at Trenton and entering the State of Pennsylvania, proceeds in a generally southwesterly direction toward Philadelphia. The road surface between Trenton and Philadelphia will be found hard-surfaced the entire distance. Public interest in the Lincoln Highway in Pennsylvania has been great and as a result a great amount of constructive improvement has been completed. Over a half million dollars have been spent reconstructing the mountain roads and putting the route in good condition for the tourists' use. There are but 19 miles of the entire Lincoln Highway in the State that are not hard-surfaced. At various points along the Lincoln Highway, tourists will find toll gates. The only toll charges on the Lincoln Highway between the two coasts are in this state, and these undoubtedly will be of short duration, since an active campaign is now being conducted toward their elimination. All of the Lincoln Highway Consuls are working to this end, and the active support of the Governor and the Pennsylvania State Public Service Commissioners is being received.

Twenty-four miles an hour is the maximum rate of speed on any public highway in Pennsylvania and 15 miles per hour is the speed generally allowed.

Numerous grade crossings will be found where care should be exercised in driving. These in turn are to be eliminated as soon as possible by the State authorities.

The Lincoln Highway across the Alleghany Mountains from Chambersburg to Bedford has been entirely reconstructed and what was once a very bad road full of water breaks, is now rebuilt and no such conditions are encountered.

OXFORD VALLEY

N.Y. **S.F.** Pop. 283. Bucks County.
70 **3261** No tourist accommodations.

2

GLEN LAKE

N.Y. **S.F.** Bucks County.
72 **3259** No tourist accommodations.

1

LANGHORNE

N.Y. **S.F.** Pop. 1,000. Southern part of Bucks County.
73 **3258** Two hotels, 2 garages. Local speed limit, 4-15 miles per hour, enforced. One bank, 1 railroad, 65 general business places, 2 express companies, 2 telephone companies, 1
5 newspaper, 4 public schools, electric lights, trolley and water works.

47

Pennsylvania

LA TRIPPE

N.Y.	S.F.	Bucks County.
78	3253	No tourist accommodations.

4

BUSTLETON

N.Y.	S.F.	Pop. 1,500. Philadelphia County. Inside the city limits
82	3249	of Philadelphia.

Two hotels, one garage. Local speed limit 15 miles per hour, enforced. One bank, 2 railroads, 30 general business places, 2 express companies, 2 telephone companies, 1 public school, electric lights and water works.

9

NORTH PHILADELPHIA STATION

N.Y.	S.F.	Philadelphia County.
91	3240	No tourist accommodations. Railroad station, telegraph, express.

3

PHILADELPHIA

N.Y.	S.F.	Pop. 1,657,810. Alt. 32 feet. County seat, Philadelphia
94	3237	County. On the Delaware River. Hotel accommodations

may be secured to meet the taste of the tourist. Garages will be found convenient to all hotels. Local speed limit, 12 miles per hour, enforced. All the express companies are represented, 2 telephone companies, 7 newspapers, Independence Hall, Congress Hall, United States Mint, Fairmount Park, containing over 3,000 acres, the largest municipal park in the world, Philadelphia Navy Yard, $25,000,000 City Hall situated in the heart of the city.

6

Philadelphia is principally distinguished as a manufacturing city, and is the third in the United States in population.

Between PHILADELPHIA and LANCASTER a number of toll gates are encountered. The road surface between these two points has been brought up to excellent condition. Macadam prevails.

The tourist proceeds in a generally westerly direction over what has been known for years as the Lancaster Pike.

OVERBROOK

N.Y.	S.F.	Philadelphia County.
100	3231	No tourist accommodations. Railroad station, telegraph, express.

2

ARDMORE

N.Y.	S.F.	Pop. 3,650. Alt. 355 feet. Montgomery County.
102	3229	One hotel, rate $3.00, American plan. One railroad, 1 express company, 2 telephone companies.

2

Pennsylvania

BRYN MAWR

N.Y. **S.F.** Pop. 4,000. Alt. 415 feet. Montgomery County.
104 **3227** One hotel, 1 railroad, 1 express company, 2 telephone companies. Seat of Bryn Mawr College, one of the leading
4 institutions of learning for women in the United States.

WAYNE

N.Y. **S.F.** Pop. 2,500. Alt. 572 feet. Delaware County.
108 **3223** Two hotels, 2 garages. Local speed limit, 20 miles per hour, enforced. One bank, 2 railroads, 16 general business
places, 1 express company, 1 telephone company, 1 news-
3 paper, 8 public schools, electric lights, trolley and water works. Commercial Club.

BERWYN

N.Y. **S.F.** Pop. 1,250. Alt. 498 feet. Chester County.
111 **3220** Manufacturing town. One railroad, 1 express company, 2 telephone companies.
2

PAOLI

N.Y. **S.F.** Pop. 400. Alt. 541 feet. Chester County.
113 **3218** Railroad station, telegraph, express. It was near this point that General Wayne was surprised and defeated by
9 the British on September 20, 1777. See Memorial Chapel at Valley Forge near here. Most beautiful spot.

WHITFORD

N.Y. **S.F.** Pop. 80. Alt. 360 feet. Chester County.
122 **3209** No hotels, no garage, 1 service station. Three toll gates in county, 2 railroads, 1 general business place, 1 public
3 school.

DOWNINGTON

N.Y. **S.F.** Pop. 3,326. Alt. 256 feet. Chester County. Situated in
125 **3206** the Chester Valley on the east branch of Brandywine Creek.
2 Two railroads, 2 express companies, 2 telephone companies, manufacturers of paper, wagons, glass, etc.

THORNDALE STATION

N.Y. **S.F.** Pop. 137. Alt. 325 feet. Chester County.
127 **3204** No tourist accommodations. Railroad station, telegraph, express.
4

COATSVILLE

N.Y. **S.F.** Pop. 15,000. Alt. 325 feet. Chester County.
131 **3200** Six hotels, seven garages. Local speed limit, 15 miles per hour, enforced. Route marked through city and county, signs at city limits. Route in excellent condition
4 clear across the county. Two railroads, 2 telephone companies, large steel and iron works, 2 railroad crossings at

Pennsylvania

grade, protected. Three banks, about 500 general business places, 2 express companies, 2 telephone companies, 2 newspapers, 10 public schools, Commercial Club. L. H. Town Consul, Hon. W. L. W. Jones, the Chief Burgess.

SADSBURYVILLE
N.Y. 135 **S.F.** 3196 — 4. Pop. 300. Chester County.
One hotel, $1.50, American. No garage. Route marked through village and county. One toll gate at eastern end of county. Five general business places, 1 telephone company, electric lights.

MT. VERNON
N.Y. 139 **S.F.** 3192 — 2. Pop. 25. Alt. 800 feet. Lancaster County.
One hotel, no garages. Route marked through village and county. Two general business places. One public school. Five toll gates between Mt. Vernon and Lancaster, toll 25 cents.

GAP
N.Y. 141 **S.F.** 3190 — 2. Pop. 1,000. Alt. 460 feet. Lancaster County.
Two hotels, two garages. Eight general business places, 1 bank, 1 public school, 1 railroad, 1 express company, 2 telephone companies, 1 trolley line, electric lights.

KINZERS
N.Y. 143 **S.F.** 3188 — 3. Pop. 195. Alt. 440 feet. Lancaster County.
One hotel, 1 railroad, 2 telephone companies, 1 express company, 5 general business places.

LEAMAN PLACE
N.Y. 146 **S.F.** 3185 — 2. Pop. 500. Alt. 390 feet. Lancaster County.
No hotels, one garage. Route marked through village and county. One railroad crossing at grade, protected. One railroad, 1 express company, 2 telephone companies, 1 general business place, 2 public schools, electric lights, 1 trolley line.

Pennsylvania

PARADISE

N.Y. **S.F.** Pop. 750. Alt. 390 feet. Lancaster County.
148 **3183** One hotel. Route marked through village and county, 1 machine and repair shop, 1 trolley line, 2 telephone companies, electric lights, 4 general business places, 3 public schools.
5

SOUDERSBURG

N.Y. **S.F.** Pop. 150. Alt. 360 feet. Lancaster County.
153 **3178** No hotels, no garages. One trolley line, 2 telephone companies, electric lights, 1 public school.
4

LANCASTER

N.Y. **S.F.** Pop. 50,000. Alt. 370 feet. County seat, Lancaster County.
157 **3174** Nine hotels, 7 garages. Local speed limit 15 miles per hour, enforced, but lenient. Route marked through city and county. Signs at city limits, 12 banks, 2 railroads, 2 express companies, 2 telephone companies, 6 newspapers, 40 public schools, Chamber of Commerce, Automobile Club. L. H. Town Consul, J. G. Forney, L. H. County Consul, Chas. M. Reiling.
7
The richest agricultural county in the United States. Great tobacco growing center.
Four toll gates between Lancaster and Columbia, toll average 2½ cents per mile, 25 cents.

Pennsylvania
LANCASTER to GETTYSBURG

The roads are of excellent to fair macadam.

MOUNTVILLE

N.Y. **S.F.** Pop. 800. Alt. 440 feet. Lancaster County.
164   **3167** Two hotels, 1 garage. Local speed limit, 15 miles per
                    hour, enforced. Route marked through city and county.
       3   Signs at city limits. One bank, 1 railroad, 1 express com-
                    pany, 2 telephone companies, 1 trolley line, electric lights
                    and water works, 5 general business places, 1 public school.

COLUMBIA

N.Y. **S.A.** Pop. 11,600. Alt. 400 feet. Lancaster County. On the Sus-
167   **3164** quehanna River.
                    Six hotels, 2 garages. Local speed limit, 15 miles per
                    hour, enforced. Two railroad crossings at grade, 4 banks,
       2   4 railroads, 153 general business places, 2 newspapers, 9
                    public schools, Commercial Club, Automobile Club. Toll
                    bridge over Susquehanna River between Columbia and
                    Wrightsville. Toll 25-40 cents.

WRIGHTSVILLE

N.Y. **S.F.** Pop. 2,051. Alt. 257 feet. York County. On the Sus-
169   **3162** quehanna River, opposite Columbia (with which it is con-
                    nected by bridge).
       11   One hotel, 1 railroad, 1 telephone company, 1 express com-
                    pany, manufactures iron, gasoline engines, hardware, lum-
                    ber, lime, prepared tobacco, etc.

Pennsylvania

YORK

N.Y.	S.F.	
180	3151	Pop. 50,000. Alt. 381 feet. County seat, York County. Thirty-three hotels, $1.50 up. Seven garages. Local speed limit 15 miles per hour, enforced. Route marked through city and county, signs at city limits. Two railroad crossings at grade, protected. Several toll gates in county, 1½c per mile. Eleven banks, 4 railroads, 2 express companies, 2 telephone companies, 3 newspapers, 23 public schools, Commercial Club, Automobile Club. Fine hard oiled road entire distance through York County. L. H. County Consul, A. P. Broomell, L. H. Town Consul, Eugene Weiser, Sec'y of Chamber of Commerce.
	15	

ABBOTTSTOWN

N.Y.	S.F.	
195	3136	Pop. 350. Adams County. One hotel, 1 garage. Route marked through village and county. One railroad crossing at grade, not protected. One toll gate in county, 1¾c per mile. One railroad, 7 general business places, 1 public school.
	4	

NEW OXFORD

N.Y.	S.F.	
199	3132	Pop. 1,000. Adams County. Two hotels, $1.50-$2.00, American. Two garages. Local speed limit, 12 miles per hour, enforced. Route marked through city and county, signs at city limits. Two railroad crossings at grade, protected. One bank, 14 business places, 1 express company, 1 telephone company, 1 newspaper, 1 public school.
	10	

Pennsylvania

GETTYSBURG

N.Y. S.F. Pop. 4,100. County seat, Adams County.

209   3122 Seven hotels, $2.00 up, American. Four garages. Local speed limit, 15 miles per hour, enforced. Route marked through city and county. Three banks, 2 railroads, 1 express company, 1 telephone company, 3 newspapers, electric lights, trolley and water works.

Scene of the greatest battle of the Civil War, July 1-3, 1863, and called the "High-water mark of the Rebellion." Guides may be obtained at the hotels and are able to give the details of the battle complete. The battle field lies mainly to the S. W. of the town and is now a Government park with fine roads all through it. There were about 80,000 men on the Union side and 73,000 men on the Confederate; 339 Union cannon against 293 Confederate. General G. G. Meade and Robert E. Lee commanded the armies. The Union loss was 23,003 and the Confederate 20,451.

GETTYSBURG to CHAMBERSBURG

There is a long, steady climb over the Alleghany Mountains. The tourist between these points travels the old

Pennsylvania

Philadelphia-Pittsburg turnpike. All of the ground between Gettysburg and Chambersburg is historic, having been fought over and camped on by both the Union and Confederate forces.

SEVEN STARS

N.Y. **S.F.** Pop. 25. Adams County.

211 **3120** No hotels, no garages. Route is marked through town and county. One railroad crossing at grade, not protected. One railroad, 2 general business places, 1 express company, 1 public school, Battlefield of Gettysburg extends

3 to within a few hundred yards of Seven Stars where first shot of the battle was fired. First battlefield monument about ⅝ mile distant to the east.

MCKNIGHTSTOWN

N.Y. **S.F.** Pop. 175. Adams County.

214 **3117** No tourist accommodations.

1

CASHTOWN

N.Y. **S.F.** Pop. 200. Adams County.

215 **3116** One hotel, no garages. Route marked through village and county, signs at village limits. Five general business

5 places, 1 public school, water works. Rock Top on mountain was used as a signal point during the Battle of Gettysburg, July, 1863.

GRAFENBURG

N.Y. **S.F.** Adams County.

220 **3111** Summer resort. No accommodations for tourists.

2

CALEDONIA PARK

N.Y. **S.F.** Franklin County.

222 **3109** No tourist accommodations.

5

FAYETTEVILLE

N.Y. **S.F.** Pop. 800. Franklin County.

227 **3104** No hotels. Route marked through town and county. One railroad crossing at grade, unprotected. One railroad, 5

2 general business places, 1 express company, 1 public school, trolley line.

WEST FAYETTEVILLE

N.Y. **S.F.** Franklin County.

229 **3102** No tourist accommodations.

4

Pennsylvania

CHAMBERSBURG

N.Y. **S.F.** Pop. 12,000. Alt. 613 feet. County seat, Franklin County.
233 **3098** Five hotels, $1.50 up, American. Five garages. Local speed limit, 15 miles per hour, enforced. Route marked through city and county, signs at city limits. One railroad crossing at grade, protected, 4 banks, 2 railroads, 3 express companies, 2 telephone companies, 3 newspapers, 6 public schools, electric lights, trolley and water works. Commercial club, Automobile Club. L. H. Town Consul, W.
7 H. Fisher.

City destroyed by Confederate Army during Civil War. See monument in square commemorating the event. The Lincoln Highway was the route traveled by the Confederate army under Lee to Gettysburg when Meade's forces were met and the battle of Gettysburg occurred.

The chief interest in this town lies in the fact that the greater part of Lee's army was in camp here, and moved from this point to the battle of Gettysburg.

Here is located the first arch erected over the Lincoln Highway.

ST. THOMAS

N.Y. **S.F.** Pop. 500. Franklin County.
240 **3091** One hotel, $1.50, American. Local speed limit 12 miles per hour, enforced. Route marked through village and county, signs at approach to town. One bank, 6 general business places, telephone exchange handles telegraph mes-
6 sages, 2 public schools.

All deeds or mortgages recorded use the name "Lincoln Highway," replacing former designation "Main Street."

FORT LOUDON

N.Y. **S.F.** Pop. 400. Franklin County.
246 **3085** One hotel, 1 garage. Local speed limit, 20 miles per hour. Route marked through town and county, signs at town limits. One railroad crossing at grade, protected. Two
8 railroads, 4 general business places, 1 express company, 1 telephone company, 1 public school.

MC CONNELLSBURG

N.Y. **S.F.** Pop. 800. County seat, Fulton County.
254 **3077** Two hotels, 3 garages. Route marked through town and county, signs at town limits. Two banks, 25 general business places, 1 telephone company, 3 newspapers, 1 public school.

6 Beautiful mountain scenery, good fishing and especially good hunting. Large state game preserve just east of town, on mountain. Many natural features of interest in the way of disorderly formations of surface, etc. Automobile Club.

HARRISONVILLE

N.Y. **S.F.** Pop. 25. Fulton County.
260 **3071** One hotel. Route marked through town and county. Bell Telephone connects with Western Union at Mc-
12 Connelsburg. One public school. Beautiful mountain scenery on all sides.

Pennsylvania

BREEZEWOOD

N.Y.	S.F.	Pop. 80. Bedford County.
272	3059	One hotel, 1 garage. Route marked through town and county. Extensive road improvement completed in 1915. One public school.
8		

EVERETT

N.Y.	S.F.	Pop. 3,000. Alt. 1,118 feet. Bedford County.
280	3051	Three hotels, $1.50 up, American. Two garages. Local speed limit, 12 miles per hour, not enforced. Route marked through city and county, signs at city limits. Extensive road improvement completed in 1915. Two banks, 2 railroads, 24 general business places, 1 express company, 2 telephone companies, 2 newspapers, 2 public schools, electric lights and water works. L. H. Local Consul, A. M. Karne.
1		

MT. DALLS

N.Y.	S.F.	Alt. 672 feet. Bedford County.
281	3050	Railroad and telegraph station. No accommodations for tourists.
3		

THE WILLOWS

N.Y.	S.F.	Bedford County.
284	3047	No tourist accommodations.
4		

Pennsylvania

BEDFORD

N.Y.	S.F.	
288	3043	
	2	

Pop. 2,500. Alt. 1,061 feet. County seat, Bedford County. Nine hotels, $1.00 up. Two garages. Local speed limit 15 miles per hour, enforced. Route marked through city and county, signs at city limits. Extensive road improvement completed in 1915. Two banks, 2 railroads, about 75 general business places, one express company, 1 telephone company, 2 newspapers, 2 public schools, electric lights and water works. Bedford Springs noted for its fine mineral waters, beautiful mountain scenery. Commercial Club. L. H. County Consul, Lee F. Hoffman.

In the heart of the Alleghany Mountains, dates back to 1776. General Washington and several thousand soldiers of the Continental Army encamped here during the Revolutionary War. An old stone house, then occupied by Washington, is still standing.

A little farther on we come to Grand View, one of the finest views in the Alleghany Mountains. This spot served as a "lookout" for the highwayman, Davie Lewis.

The Lincoln Highway through here was originally laid out by Washington when following his profession of surveyor.

BEDFORD to PITTSBURG

The tourist proceeds over the old Philadelphia-Pittsburg turnpike. The roads between these two points are all in excellent

Pennsylvania

condition now, the majority of the surface being macadam. The country is quite mountainous and care should be exercised. This means especial attention to tires, brakes, etc.

The tourists' attention is called to the magnificent view obtained at Point Lookout, which is unsurpassed by any bit of scenic splendor to be found anywhere in the country.

WOLFSBURG

N.Y.	S.F.	
290	3041	Pop. 170. Alt. 1,097 feet. Bedford County.
		No tourist accommodations. Route marked through town and county. One express company, 1 public
7		school, 2 stores, flour mill, blacksmith shop and cigar factory and other small industries, 1 railroad.

SCHELLBURG

N.Y.	S.F.	
297	3034	Pop. 350. Bedford County.
		One hotel, 1 garage. Local speed limit, 18 miles per hour, enforced. Route marked through town and
12		county, signs at Borough limits. One bank, 4 general business places, 1 public school.

BUCKSTOWN

N.Y.	S.F.	
309	3022	Pop. 125. Somerset County.
		No tourist accommodations. Gas and oil can be purchased in the village. Route marked through village
4		and county. Two trolley lines.

KANTER P. O.

N.Y.	S.F.	
313	3018	Pop. 177. Somerset County.
		No tourist accommodations.
3		

STOYESTOWN

N.Y.	S.F.	
316	3015	Pop. 400. Somerset County. Midway between the Laurel Hill Mountain and the Alleghany Mountains.
		Two hotels, 2 garages. Local speed limit, 15 miles per hour, enforced. Route marked through village and
7		county, signs at village limits. Four railroad crossings at grade, signs at all crossings. One bank, 3 railroads, 4 general business places, 1 express company, 2 public schools, electric lights, trolley and water works. Beautiful mountain scenery.

JENNERS

N.Y.	S.F.	
323	3008	Somerset County.
		No tourist accommodations. Railroad station, telegraph.
1		

JENNERSTOWN

N.Y.	S.F.	
324	3007	Pop. 300. Somerset County.
		One hotel, 1 garage. Route marked through village and county. Extensive road improvement completed in 1915.
8		Eight railroads, 2 business places, 1 public school.

Pennsylvania

MC LAUGHLINTOWN

N.Y. **S.F.** Westmoreland County.
332 **2999** No tourist accommodations.

3

LIGONIER

N.Y. **S.F.** Pop. 2,000. Westmoreland County.
335 **2996** Four hotels, 2 garages. Route marked through city and county. Arches have been built at the city limits. Two railroad crossings at grade, unprotected. Two banks,
9 2 railroads. 30 general business places, 1 express company, 2 newspapers, 1 public school, electric lights and water works. Beautiful scenery.

YOUNGSTOWN

N.Y. **S.F.** Pop. 323. Alt. 852 feet. Westmoreland County. No
344 **2987** tourist accommodations.

10

GREENSBURG

N.Y. **S.F.** Pop. 14,687. Alt. 1,086 feet. County seat, Westmoreland
354 **2977** County. Nine hotels, rates $1.00 up. Garages in connection with many of the hotels. One railroad, 1 express
4 company, 1 telephone company. Greensburg manufactures glass, engines, flour, etc. It is a coal and gas region.

GRAPEVILLE

N.Y. **S.F.** Pop. 210. Alt. 1,060 feet. Westmoreland County.
358 **2973** Railroad station, 1 express company, 1 telephone company. No tourist accomodations.
2

ADAMSBURG

N.Y. **S.F.** Pop. 300. Westmoreland County.
360 **2971** No tourist accommodations. Railroad station, telegraph.

3

IRWIN

N.Y. **S.F.** Pop. 2,886. Alt. 881 feet. Westmoreland County.
363 **2968** One hotel, 1 railroad, 1 express company, 2 telephone companies, foundries, etc. Here are some of the most
1 extensive coal mines in the state.

JACKSONVILLE

N.Y. **S.F.** Westmoreland County.
364 **2967** No tourist accommodations.

6

Pennsylvania

EAST MC KEESPORT

N.Y. **S.F.** Pop. 3,500. Allegheny County.

370 **2961** One hotel, 1 garage. Local speed limit, 15 miles per hour, enforced. Route marked through city and county, signs at city limits. Twenty-five general business places, 2 public **2** schools, electric lights, 1 interurban line, water works. Extensive road improvement completed in 1915.

TURTLE CREEK

N.Y. **S.F.** Pop. 4,995. Alt. 749 feet. Allegheny County. On Turtle **372** **2959** Creek. Three railroads, 3 express companies, telegraph. **1**

EAST PITTSBURG

N.Y. **S.F.** Pop. 6,500. Allegheny County.

373 **2958** Thirteen hotels, one garage. Local speed limit 15 miles per hour, enforced. Route marked through city and county. One bank, 2 railroads, 30 general business places, **4** 3 express companies, 2 telephone companies, 2 public schools, electric lights and trolley. Commercial Club.

WILKINSBURG

N.Y. **S.F.** Pop. 20,000. Alt. 922 feet. Allegheny County.

377 **2954** Six garages, 4 banks, over 200 general business places, 2 express companies, 2 telephone companies, 2 newspapers, 6 **7** public schools. Commercial Club. Automobile Club. Immediate suburb of Pittsburg.

PITTSBURG

N.Y. **S.F.** Pop. 600,000. Alt. 745 feet. County seat, Allegheny County.

384 **2947** Situated at the junction of the Allegheny and Mononga-hela rivers, where they unite to form the Ohio. Seventeen hotels. Pittsburg has one of the largest convention halls in the country. Pittsburg ranks fifth in commercial and industrial importance among the cities of the United States. It is the center of iron, steel and glass industries, and also the largest shipping point for bituminous coal. **23** Pittsburg's coal district embraces an era of 14,000 square miles. Has well paved streets, splendid boulevards, a system of parks. Has 14 hospitals and 80 charities, a well-equipped educational system, which includes 87 ward and 3 high schools. Pittsburg is the largest manufacturing center for iron and steel in the world. An interesting feature of Pittsburg to the tourist is the "Block House," part of the original Fort Pitt, which is maintained in a good state of preservation, near the Point.

PITTSBURG to BEAVER

Between Pittsburg and Beaver the tourist will find improved pavement entire route. Highway well marked. Leaving Pittsburg the route follows the main streets of several small boroughs to Sewickley. Three dangerous grade crossings protected by watchman until late at night. Speed limit generally 15 miles p. h.

[Pennsylvania

LEETSDALE

N.Y. **S.F.** Pop. 1,904. Alt. 714 feet. Allegheny County. On the
407 **2924** Ohio River.

Railroad station, 2 express companies, 1 telephone com-
1 pany.

FAIROAKS

N.Y. **S.F.** Pop. 225. Allegheny County.
408 **2923** No tourist accommodations. Railroad station, telegraph,
express.
1

AMBRIDGE

N.Y. **S.F.** Pop. 7,000. Beaver County. On the Ohio River. Three
409 **2922** hotels, 3 garages, 1 bank, 1 railroad, 1 express company, 1
telephone company, 2 newspapers, 5 public schools, electric
1 lights, trolley and water works. Commercial Club.

ECONOMY

N.Y. **S.F.** Pop. 900. Alt. 714 feet. Beaver County. On the Ohio
410 **2921** River. One railroad, 2 express companies, 1 telephone company. Economy was founded by the "Harmonists" in 1825,
1 after their return from Indiana.

LEGIONVILLE

N.Y. **S.F.** Pop. 25. Beaver County.
411 **2920** No tourist accommodations. Railroad station, telegraph.

This is the site of the encampment during the winter
of 1792-93, of "Mad Anthony" Wayne's army known as
"The Legion of the United States." Here he went into
winter quarters, and the following spring won his
1 brilliant and epoch-making victory over the Indians of
the Miami Confederation in the battle of Fallen
Timbers. Wayne was appointed by Washington to
the command of the army of the United States at the
close of the Revolutionary War.

LOGANS

N.Y. **S.F.** Alt. 512 feet. Beaver County.
412 **2919** Only a railroad station. No accommodations for tourists.

1

BADEN

N.Y. **S.F.** Pop. 800. Alt. 673 feet. Beaver County. On the Ohio
413 **2918** River.

Gas and oil can be purchased. Local speed limit 15 miles
per hour, enforced. One railroad, 3 general business places,
1 1 express company, 1 telephone company, 1 public school,
electric lights, trolley and water works.

Pennsylvania

CONWAY

N.Y. S.F. Pop. 1,483. Alt. 704 feet. Beaver County.
414 2917 Two railroads, telegraph.

1   Conway, is the location of the largest railroad yards in the country, owned by the Pennsylvania Railroad Company.

FREEDOM

N.Y. S.F. Pop. 4,000. Alt. 703 feet. Beaver County. On the Ohio
415 2916 River.

2   Two hotels. Local speed limit, 15 miles per hour. Route marked through city. One railroad crossing at grade, protected. Two banks, 3 railroads, 26 general business places, 1 express company, 1 telephone company, 3 public schools, electric lights, water works, 1 interurban line. Commercial Club.

ROCHESTER

N.Y. S.F. Pop. 5903. Alt. 705 feet. Beaver County. On the Ohio
417 2914 River.

1   Three hotels, two garages. Local speed limit, 15 miles per hour, enforced. Route marked through city and county. One railroad crossing at grade, protected. Three railroads, 2 express companies, 1 telephone company, 30 public schools, electric lights, trolley and water works. Automobile Club and Commercial Club.

     The famous Chief Logan, of the Mingo Tribe, had his home at this point, and it was consequently the rendezvous of various Indian tribes.

     The largest cut-glass plant in the United States is now situated at this place.

BRIDGEWATER

N.Y. S.F. Pop. 1,562. Alt. 736 feet. Beaver County. At the junction
418 2913 of the Beaver and Ohio Rivers.

1   Route is marked through city and county. Local speed limit, 15 miles per hour, enforced. The tourist passes over the mouth of what is to be the Ohio River and Lake Erie Ship Canal, thus making a water way shipping feature around the world. Rochester, Bridgewater and Beaver being co-terminous, the tourist accommodations are the same.

     Here is the scene of Aaron Burr's operations in carrying out his great conspiracy for the establishment of an empire in the Southwest.

     The first steamboat plying the Ohio River was built here.

BEAVER

N.Y. S.F. Pop. 4,300. Alt. 748 feet. County seat, Beaver County.
419 2912 Junction of the Beaver and Ohio Rivers.

10   One hotel, 3 garages. Local speed limit, 15 miles per hour, enforced. Route marked through city and county, signs at city limits. Three banks, 3 railroads, 2 express companies, 1 telephone company, 1 newspaper, 3 public schools, electric lights, trolley and water works. L. H. Town Consul, Chas. Henry Stone. County Consul, H. O. Allison.

Pennsylvania

This is the site of Old Fort McIntosh, where, in 1785, a treaty of peace was signed with the Delaware, Wyandotte, Chippewa and Ottawa Indians. It is historically known for the battles between the Indians and the whites which were fought in this vicinity.

The town is situated on the plateau at the junction of the Ohio and Beaver Rivers. The route of the $50,000,000 ship canal goes via the Beaver River to Lake Erie.

BEAVER to EAST LIVERPOOL

The roads between these points (18 miles of t' distance is the only unimproved section in Pennsylvania), will found fair to poor, depending largely upon the weather cond .is. Much grading, dragging, and rolling have been instituted. At certain points the roads will be found to be narrow. This ro. .e is scheduled for early improvement by the State of Pennsylvania under the terms of the Sproul Act, which will make it one of the most beautiful drives in the State of Pennsylvania . The road follows the ridge route of the Tuscarawas Indian Trail.

ESTHER

N.Y.   S.F. Pop. 150. Beaver County.

429   2902 Route marked through town and county.

2

OHIOVILLE

N.Y.   S.F. Pop. 25. Beaver County.

431   2900 No tourist accommodations.

4

SMITH'S FERRY

N.Y.   S.F. Pop. 580. Beaver County. On the Ohio River.

435   2896 One railroad, 1 express company, 1 telephone company.

5 The town was founded in 1792, and near the village, on the left bank of the Ohio River, are large rocks upon which Indian carvings may yet be seen.

Gasolene and Oil Storage Outfits

Will supply the life blood of your automobile at every stopping point on the Lincoln Highway.

Now there must be a reason for such unusual use of Bowser Equipment. The reason is—Quality first, last, and all the time.

It is evidence that autoists have known ever since the first automobile toured, that a Bowser Outfit stands Sentry for pure, full-powered, full-measured, filtered "gas" and clean, velvety, full-measured lubricants.

On the Road or at Home use a

BOWSER

A Bowser Outfit is an unwritten guarantee that the owner has uppermost in his mind, service to his trade.

Write us for illustrated literature explaining why Bowser Systems are efficient and economical for Public, Private and Commercial Garages.

When in the neighborhood of Fort Wayne visit our factory and actually tour through it in your car.

S. F. BOWSER & CO., Inc., Fort Wayne, Ind.
Sales Offices in all Centers and Representatives Everywhere

Ohio

L. H. STATE CONSUL, J. E. HOPLEY,
Bucyrus, Ohio

GENERAL INFORMATION

THE route of the Lincoln Highway across Ohio is completely marked, and rapid progress is being made both in hard-surfacing the road and in the building of concrete bridges replacing the old wooden structures. There are 66 miles of brick and 111 miles of other hard-surfacing on the Lincoln Highway in the State and more than $1,256,780.00 was spent in improvements during the last 18 months. Between 70 and 80 per cent of the entire Lincoln Highway in Ohio will be found hard-surfaced. The stretches of country road vary from excellent to poor in a few locations. Ohio has 244 miles of Lincoln Highway.

The laws of Ohio relating to the speed of motor cars demand 8 miles per hour in the business or closely built-up portions of a municipality; 15 miles per hour in other portions of a municipality, and 20 miles per hour outside a municipality. It is further stated that no vehicle shall operate on a road at a speed greater than reasonable or proper or so as to endanger the property, life or limb of any person.

EAST LIVERPOOL

N.Y. **S.F.** Pop. 23,000. Alt. 692 feet. Columbiana County. On the
440 **2891** Ohio River.

Five hotels, 6 garages. State law governs local speed limit, enforced. Route marked through city and county. Five banks, 1 railroad, 300 general business places, 2 express companies, 2 telephone companies, 2 newspapers, 16 public schools, electric lights, 2 trolley lines, municipal water works, Commercial Organizations, Booster Club, H. B. Barth, Commissioner, Lincoln Highway Consul, Frank D. Swaney.

15 This city is the center of the pottery industry of the United States.

The Confederate General John H. Morgan's command captured near here during the Civil War, the farthest northern point reached by any body of Confederate soldiers.

This city is located in the most scenic section of the middle west. The states of Ohio, Pennsylvania and West Virginia converge on an island opposite the east end of the city.

LISBON

N.Y. **S.F.** Pop, 4,000. County Seat, Columbiana County.
455 **2876** Two hotels, 3 garages. Local speed limit 15 miles per hour, enforced. Route marked through city and county. Extensive road improvement completed in 1915. One railroad crossing at grade, unprotected. Two banks, 1 railroad about 75 general business places, 2 express companies, 1 telephone company, 3 newspapers, 2 public schools,
9 electric lights and water works. Manufacturing district,

Ohio

surrounding country producing coal, lime and fire clay. Commercial Club. L. H. County Consul, Clark B. Firestone. Local Consuls, W. H. Hepburn and John Patterson.

Lisbon is with one exception, the oldest town in Ohio, having been founded in 1804. The old McKinley furnace is in the northwestern part of the town and was operated by President McKinley's father.

A monument, seven miles south of here, marks the site of the surrender of the rebel raider, John Morgan.

HANOVERTON

N.Y.	S.F.	Pop. 325. Columbiana County.
464	2867	Two hotels, 2 garages. Local speed limit 8 miles per hour, enforced. Route marked through village and county, signs at limits of town. Seven general business places, 1 public school.
	1	

KENSINGTON

N.Y.	S.F.	Pop. 350. Alt. 1,115 feet. Columbiana County.
465	2866	One hotel, 1 garage. Local speed limit 20 miles per hour, enforced. Route marked through town and county. One bank, 2 railroads, 14 general business places, 1 express company, 1 telephone company, 1 public school, 1 trolley line. L. H. Local Consul, Frank Cox.
	5	

EAST ROCHESTER

N.Y.	S.F.	Pop. 250. Columbiana County.
470	2861	No tourist accommodations. Railroad station, 1 express company.
	3	

MINERVA

N.Y.	S.F.	Pop. 2,000. Alt. 1,050 feet. Stark County.
473	2858	Two hotels, 2 garages. Local speed limit 15 miles per hour, enforced. Route marked through city and county. Two banks, 3 railroads 91 general business places, 3 express companies, 1 telephone company, 1 newspaper, 1 public school, electric lights, and water works. Tableware and special pottery. Highland Milk Condensery, capacity 150,000 lbs. of milk per day, flour mill, paving brick and fire-proofing, hardware, specialties, furniture, lumber, cooperage. Commercial Club, Auto Club. L. H. Local Consul, Willard Pennock.
	6	

ROBERTSVILLE

N.Y.	S.F.	Pop. 267. Stark County.
479	2852	Tourist accommodations. Railroad station, 1 express company.
	6	

OSNABURG

N.Y.	S.F.	Pop. 650. Stark County.
485	2846	One hotel, 1 garage, 1 railroad, crossing at grade not protected. One railroad, 6 general business places, 1 express company, 1 telephone company, 1 public school, electric lights.
	5	

Ohio

CANTON

N.Y. **S.F.** Pop. 60,000. Alt. 1,031 feet. County seat, Stark County.

490 **2841** Six hotels, rates $1.50 up. Ten garages. Local speed limit 15 miles per hour, enforced. Route marked through city and county. Extensive road improvement completed in 1915. Three railroad crossings at grade, protected. Nine banks, 3 railroads, 250 general business places, 3 express companies, 2 telephone companies, 2 newspapers, 18 public schools, $500,000 McKinley Monument and burial place of Ex-President and Mrs. McKinley. Commercial Club, L. H. County Consul, J. A. Kress, L. H. Local Consul, Lewis H. Fogle.

8

CANTON to LIMA

The tourist along this section will find all types of road improvement, much of which is brick, some concrete and some macadam. The tourist will note many attempts to keep the dirt roads in satisfactory condition by dragging.

MASSILLON

N.Y. **S.F.** Pop. 16,000. Alt. 952 feet. Stark County.

498 **2833** One hotel, 8 garages. Local speed limit, 8-15 miles per hour, enforced. Route marked through city and county. Three railroad crossings at grade, protected. Seven banks, 4 railroads, 150 general business places, 3 express companies, 2 telephone companies, 1 newspaper, 11 public schools. Commercial Club, Automobile Club. L. H. Local Consuls, A. B. Altland and Fred W. Justus.

2

WEST BROOKFIELD

N.Y. **S.F.** Pop. 300. Stark County.

500 **2831** No tourist accommodations. L. H. Local Consul, David Leavens.

3

EAST GREENVILLE

N.Y. **S.F.** Pop. 250. Stark County.

503 **2828** No accommodations for tourists. Route marked through town and county. One trolley line.

4

DALTON

N.Y. **S.F.** Pop. 600. Alt. 1,050 feet. Wayne County.

507 **2824** One hotel, $1.00 American. One garage. Local speed limit, 8 miles per hour, enforced. Route marked through town and county. One railroad. 1 express company, 1 telephone company. L. H. Local Consul, T. C. Hunsicker.

7

EAST UNION

N.Y. **S.F.** Pop. 25. Wayne County.

514 **2817** No tourist accommodations. Railroad station.

6

Ohio

WOOSTER

N.Y. **S.F.** Pop. 6,136. Alt. 901 feet. County seat, Wayne County.

520 **2811** Three hotels, $2.00 up. Five garages. Local speed limit, 8-18 miles per hour, enforced. Route marked through city and county, signs at city limits. Two express companies, 2 telephone companies, Wooster College, the Ohio Agricultural Experimental Station.

4

City is situated in the midst of a fine grain growing and agricultural district. L. H. County Consul, Emmet C. Dix; L. H. Local Consul, Donald Foss.

JEFFERSON

N.Y. **S.F.** Wayne County.

524 **2807** No tourist accommodations.

5

NEW PITTSBURG

N.Y. **S.F.** Pop. 250. Wayne County.

529 **2802** No accommodations for tourists. Route marked through town and county, signs at town limits. Road improvement completed in 1915. Two general business places, 1 public school.

4

ROWSBURG

N.Y. **S.F.** Pop. 250. Ashland County.

533 **2798** One hotel $2.00 American. Route marked through town and county, signs at town limits. Two general business places, 1 public school.

9

ASHLAND

N.Y. **S.F.** Pop. 10,000. Alt. 1,076 feet. County seat, Ashland County.

542 **2789** One hotel, $2.00 American. Three fine restaurants, 6 garages. Local speed limit, 8-15 mile per hour, enforced. Route marked through city and county, signs at city limits. Three banks, 3 railroads, 111 general business places, 2 express companies, 3 newspapers, 9 public schools, Chamber of Commerce, Commercial Club, Automobile Club. L. H. County Consul, J. L. Clark.

·14

MANSFIELD

N.Y. **S.F.** Pop. 25,000. Alt. 1,151 feet. County seat Richland County.

556 **2775** Four hotels, $1.50 up, American. Six garages. Local speed limit, 8-15 miles per hour, enforced. Route marked through city and county. Extensive road improvement completed in 1915. One railroad crossing at grade protected. Seven banks, 3 railroads, 3 express companies, 3 telephone companies, 3 newspapers, 10 public schools. Ohio State Reformatory. L. H. County Consul, T. R. Barnes.

8

ONTARIO

N.Y. **S.F.** Pop. 250. Alt. 1,373 feet. Richland County.

564 **2767** No tourist accommodations. Three railroads, 3 general business places, 1 public school, interurban line, electric lights and water works.

5

The road between Mansfield and Galion was completely improved for travel during 1915.

Ohio

GALION

N.Y. **S.F.**
569 **2762**

14

Pop. 8,200. Alt. 1,167 feet. Crawford County.

Two hotels, two garages. Local speed limit, 8 miles per hour, enforced. Extensive road improvement completed during 1915. Route marked through city and county. Two railroad crossings at grade, protected. Three banks, 8 railroads, 2 newspapers, 4 public schools, 2 express companies, 1 telephone company, 250 general business places, electric lights, trolley and water works. Commercial Club, Automobile Club. L. H. Local Consul, Dr. C. D. Morgan.

BUCYRUS

N.Y. **S.F.**
583 **2748**

8

Pop. 9,103. Alt. 1,003 feet. County seat, Crawford County.

Four hotels, six garages. Local speed limit is 8-15 miles per hour, but the tourist is merely expected to drive with due precaution. Route marked through city, signs at city limits. Four banks, 3 railroads, 320 general business places, 2 express companies, 2 telephone companies, 4 newspapers, 5 public schools, electric lights, two electric roads, water works. Commercial Club, Automobile Club, Motor-cycle Club. L. H. State Consul, John E. Hopley; L. H. County Consul, Hon. E. J. Songer, the Mayor.

NEVADA

N.Y. **S.F.**
591 **2740**

8

Pop. 889. Alt. 917 feet. Wyandot County.

One hotel, 3 restaurants, 2 garages. Route marked through town and county, signs at town limits. Five miles of new water bound road built from Nevada, in 1915. More improvements planned for 1916. Two banks, 1 railroad, 40 general business places, 1 express company, 1 telephone company, 1 newspaper, 1 public school. Commercial Club, Automobile Club. L. H. Local Consul, Dr. S. S. Barrett.

UPPER SANDUSKY

N.Y. **S.F.**
599 **2732**

13

Pop. 3,776. Alt. 850 feet. County seat, Wyandot County.

Three hotels, 4 garages (2 on the Lincoln Highway). Local speed limit, 8 miles per hour, enforced. Route marked through city and county, signs at city limits. Two railroad crossings at grade, protected. Three banks, 8 railroads, 1 express company, 2 telephone companies, Public Library, 50 general business places, 2 newspapers, 3 public schools, Parochial school, electric lights and water works. Commercial Club. L. H. County Consul, Hon. Samuel J. Black.

FOREST

N.Y. **S.F.**
612 **2719**

8

Pop. 1,500. Alt. 927 feet. Hardin County.

Two hotels, $1.50, American. Two good restaurants, 2 garages. Local speed limit, 8 miles per hour, enforced. Route marked through town and county, signs at town limits. Two railroad crossings at grade, protected. Two banks, 2 railroads, 23 general business places, 2 express companies, 1 telephone company, 1 newspaper, 2 public schools, electric lights. Commercial Club. L. H. Local Consul, C. S. Simpson.

Ohio

DUNKIRK

N.Y. **S.F.** Pop. 1,200. Hardin County.

620 **2711** Two hotels, 2 garages. Route marked through town and county, signs at town limits. Two railroads, 50 general business places, 2 express companies, 1 telephone company, 1 public school, electric lights and water works. Commercial Club. L. H. Local Consul, Omer B. Johnson.

4

DOLA

N.Y. **S.F.** Pop. 200. Hardin County.

624 **2707** One hotel, $1.00, American. One garage. Route marked through town and county. One railroad, 5 general business places, 1 express company, 1 telephone company, 1 public school.

6

ADA

N.Y. **S.F.** Pop. 3,000. Alt. 952 feet. Hardin County.

630 **2701** Two hotels, 3 garages. Local speed limit, 8-15 miles per hour, enforced. Route marked through city and county, signs at city limits. One railroad crossing at grade, protected. Two banks, 1 railroad, 60 general business places, 1 express company, 1 telephone company, 2 newspapers, 2 public schools, electric lights and water works. Commercial Club. L. H. County Consul, Justin Brewer.

16

The home town of his Excellency, the Governor of Ohio, whose residence faces the Lincoln Highway.

LIMA

N.Y. **S.F.** Pop. 42,604. Alt. 872 feet. County seat, Allen County.

646 **2685** Five hotels, rates $1.00 up. Four garages. Local speed limit, 8-15 miles per hour, enforced. Route marked through city and county. Roads in excellent condition. Three railroad crossings at grade, protected. Six railroads, 2 interurbans, 4 express companies, 2 telephone companies, electric lights and water works. L. H. Local Consul, Eugene C. Eppley. Local Automobile Club maintains a touring bureau in the lobby of the Lima House, to which all tourists are invited. Best route to Cleveland is via Findlay, Fostoria, Tiffin, Norwalk, and fine pike from there into Cleveland.

8

LIMA to FORT WAYNE

Between Lima and Van Wert the tourist will find excellent stone and gravel roads.

GOMER

N.Y. **S.F.** Pop. 200. Allen County.

654 **2677** One hotel. Route marked. One railroad, 1 express company, L. H. Local Consuls, Dr. O. S. Roebuck and G. W. Williams.

8

Ohio

DELPHOS

N.Y. **S.F.** Pop. 6,000. Alt. 776 feet. Allen County.

662 **2669** Two hotels, 6 garages. Local speed limit, 8 miles per hour. Route marked through city and county, signs at city limits. One railroad crossing at grade, protected. Three banks, 4 railroads, 1 interurban line, 150 to 200 general business places, 4 express companies, 1 telephone company, 2 newspapers, 4 public schools. Public build-

13 ings, and parks, paved street, electric lights and water works. Foundries, railroad shops, straw board and fur- niture works, metal stamping works, printing press fac- tories, electric power plant furnishing power to all cities and villages within a radius of 20 miles. Commercial Club. L. H. Local Consul, A. B. King.

VAN WERT

N.Y. **S.F.** Pop. 8,000. Alt. 782 feet. County seat, Van Wert County.

675 **2656** Five hotels, 2 garages. Local speed limit, 8-15 miles per hour, enforced. Route marked through city and county. Two railroad crossings at grade, protected. Three banks, 2 railroads, 1 interurban, 200 to 300 general business places, 2 express companies, 1 telephone company, 3 newspapers, 4 public schools, electric lights, trolley and water works. Commercial Club. L. H. County Consul, T. C. Wilkinson. Daughters of American Revolution have erected arches. Magnificent Y. W. C. A. and Y. M.

33 C. A. buildings just completed at a cost of $100,000 each.

In traveling the Lincoln Highway through Van Wert County, the tourist traverses for a distance the Ridge Road, which runs along near the crest of a natural ridge, which at one time formed the southern shore of Lake Erie. This ridge is from 5 to 10 feet higher than the land upon either side and was formed by the receding of the great glacier which covered a large part of Ohio. This ridge was for many years a favorite home and highway for the Indians in their journies east and west.

VAN WERT, OHIO to FORT WAYNE, INDIANA

Eight miles of stone; 13 miles dirt; 5 miles gravel; 7 miles concrete.

The Concrete Road

Ties Town and Country Together

THE health of the city and the wealth of the country depend on always keeping open the connecting highways.

The road of concrete is open for business and pleasure to all classes of traffic in all sorts of weather.

Satisfactory construction demands careful selection of all materials.

Use Lehigh, the National Cement.

LEHIGH
CEMENT

Indiana

LINCOLN HIGHWAY STATE CONSUL, W. M. GRIFFIN,
Fort Wayne, Indiana

GENERAL INFORMATION

INDIANA is rapidly hard-surfacing the Lincoln Highway with concrete in accordance with the specifications of the Lincoln Highway Association. To date, five of the eight counties in that state crossed by the route have spent $871,000.00. The tourist will find approximately 70 miles of hard-surfacing over the Lincoln Highway in the State and in addition some sections of the road are brick paved. Indiana is one of the first states in the Union in the development of its road system and that section of the Lincoln Highway not covered by the notation above will be found of well maintained native gravel with some stretches of macadam. The major part of the improvement completed to date will be found near Fort Wayne, South Bend and Elkhart.

Indiana asks that her visiting motorists do not drive at a greater speed than a reasonable or prudent—10 miles an hour where the buildings are close together, 15 miles per hour through the residential sections of any incorporated town or village and up to 25 miles an hour on the country road. Greater speed than 25 miles an hour is regarded as prima facie evidence that the driver is running at an unreasonable speed.

FORT WAYNE

N.Y. **S.F.** Pop. 75,000. Alt. 782 feet. County seat, Allen County.
708 **2623** Eight hotels, 8 garages. Local speed limit, 8-15 miles per hour, enforced. Route marked through city and county, signs at city limits. Extensive road improvements completed in 1915. Two railroad crossings at grade, protected. Ten banks, 7 railroads, 5 interurban lines, 4 express companies, 2 telephone companies, 4 newspapers, electric lights, trolley and water works, Commercial Club. L. H. State Consul, W. M. Griffin.

The region, of which Fort Wayne is the center, is rich in early frontier history. The flags of three nations—France, England and the United States—have floated over it. It was the scene of bitter strife during the Revolutionary War and the War of 1812, and down

14 through the years that followed, the settlers were constantly harassed by the Indians, many massacres taking place in this vicinity.

The place is named after General Anthony Wayne (Mad Anthony). A French fort—Post Miami—was located here as early as 1680.

Fort Wayne was erected in 1794 by Wayne himself. Following the massacre of the garrison of Fort Dearborn (Chicago) in 1812, the famous Chief Tecumseh planned an attack on Fort Wayne and had the place nearly starved out when General Harrison—the hero of Tippecanoe—arrived with his troops and put an end

Indiana

to the siege; destroying the village of the Indians and finally crushing their hopes of staying the advance of the white people. The last block-house of the fort remained standing until 1856.

FORT WAYNE to SOUTH BEND

The tourist along this section of the Lincoln Highway will encounter various types of road including brick, concrete and gravel, all in excellent condition for travel.

In Fort Wayne the Lincoln Highway tourist will pass over the new $200,000.00 Lincoln Highway bridge over the St. Mary's River. This beautiful structure is a standard type of the excellent results obtained in artistic and substantial building encouraged in the development of the Lincoln Highway. It may be noted that concrete and steel bridges are rapidly taking place of the old wooden structures in all of the states crossed by the Highway. The Lincoln Highway Association offers to any community building such structures the co-operation of a committee of the members of the American Institute of Architects who gratuitously donate their services to the Association that any such building endeavor may be standardized, of the highest type, and in the best of taste.

CHURUBUSCO

N.Y. S.F. Pop. 1,000. Whitley County.

722 2609 One hotel, 2 garages. Route marked through town and county, signs at town limits. One railroad crossing at grade, not protected. Two banks, 1 railroad, 3 general **9** business places, 1 express company, 1 telephone company, 2 newspapers, 1 public school, electric lights and water works. Commercial Club. L. H. Local Consul, Dr. F. B. Weaver.

MERRIAM (Noblesville)

N.Y. S.F. Pop. 80. Noble County.

731 2600 No tourist accommodations.

3

WOLF LAKE

N.Y. S.F. Pop. 500. Noble County.

734 2597 One hotel, 1 garage. Route marked through town and county. Eight general business places, 1 public school. **5** L. H. Local Consul, Dr. J. E. Luckey.

KIMMELL

N.Y. S.F. Pop. 300. Noble County.

739 2592 One hotel, 1 garage. Route marked through town and county, signs at town limits. One railroad, 6 general bus- **6** iness places, 1 express company, 1 telephone company, 1 public school.

Indiana

LIGONIER

N.Y. **S.F.**
745 **2586**

8

Pop. 2,500. Alt. 885 feet. Noble County. On the Elkhart River.

One hotel, two garages. Local speed limit, 10 miles per hour. Route marked through city and county. Extensive road improvement completed in 1915. Four banks, 1 railroad, 90 general business places, 1 express company, 2 telephone companies, 2 newspapers, 2 public schools, electric lights, and water works. Commercial Club. L. H. Local Consul, J. B. Schutt, Mayor.

BENTON

N.Y. **S.F.**
753 **2578**
10

Pop. 600. Elkhart County.

One hotel, 1 garage, 1 railroad, telephone and telegraph, 1 express company.

GOSHEN

N.Y. **S.F.**
763 **2568**

9

Pop. 10,000. Alt. 796 feet. County seat, Elkhart County. Three hotels, four garages. Local speed limit 8-12-15 miles per hour, enforced. Route marked through city and county, signs at city limits. Extensive road improvement completed in 1915. One railroad crossing at grade, protected. Four banks, 2 railroads, 2 interurban lines, 150 general business places, 2 express companies, 2 telephone companies, 2 newspapers, 7 public schools, electric lights, trolley and water works. Commercial Club. L. H. Local Consul, George M. Richardson.

Indiana

ELKHART

N.Y. **S.F.**
772 **2559**

6

Pop. 22,000. Alt. 725 feet. Elkhart County. On St. Joseph River.

Four hotels, 9 garages. Local speed limit 10-15 miles per hour, enforced. Route marked through city and county, signs at city limits. Extensive road improvement completed in 1915. One railroad crossing at grade, protected. Four banks, 3 railroads, 2 interurban lines, 300 general business places, 3 express companies, 2 telephone companies, 2 newspapers, 11 public schools, parks, electric lights, trolley and water works. Commercial Club and Automobile Club. L. H. County Consul, E. L. Arnold. Road follows the beautiful St. Joseph River.

OSCEOLA

N.Y. **S.F.**
778 **2553**

4

Pop. 250. Alt. 736 feet. St. Joseph County.

No tourist accommodations. Local speed limit 10 and 15 miles per hour, enforced. Route marked through town and county, signs at town limits. One railroad crossing at grade. One railroad, 1 electric line, 4 general business places, 1 express company, 1 telephone company, 1 public school.

The tourist will note in traveling this section of the Highway, fine concrete roads of recent construction, a development which can be traced to the active interest of the people in the Lincoln Highway propaganda. Indiana has no State Highway Commission, but has done more than any other state on the route in actual concrete construction holding to the Lincoln Highway standard. The people of northern Indiana have been quick to appreciate the benefits of hard-surfaced roads, and the idea is spreading with amazing rapidity.

MISHAWAKA

N.Y. **S.F.**
782 **2549**

4

Pop. 15,000. Alt. 726 feet. St. Joseph County.

One hotel, American plan, $1.50. One garage. Local speed limit, 10 miles per hour, enforced. Route marked through city and county, signs at city limits. Extensive road improvement completed in 1915. Three banks, 3 railroads, 2 express companies, 2 telephone companies, 1 newspaper, 4 public schools, electric lights, trolley and water works. Commercial Club.

Indiana

SOUTH BEND

N.Y.   **S.F.**   Pop. 65,114. Alt. 722 feet. County seat, St. Joseph County.
786   **2545**   On the south bank of the St. Joseph River.

Five hotels, 10 garages. Route marked through city and county, signs at city limits. Extensive road improvement completed in 1915. Two railroad crossings at grade, 11 banks, 6 railroads, 3 interurban lines, 3 express companies, 2 telephone companies, 4 newspapers, 21 public schools, parks, electric lights, trolley and water works. Commercial Club. L. H. County Consul, W. L. Kiser. Touring information at the Oliver Hotel.

16

SOUTH BEND to DYER

The major portion of this section of the Lincoln Highway is of concrete and some stretches of macadam. It is generally well maintained and will afford excellent touring.

NEW CARLISLE

N.Y.   **S.F.**   Pop. 612. Alt. 762 feet. St. Joseph County.
802   **2529**   One hotel, $1.50 American. One garage. Route marked through town and county, signs at town limits. Extensive road improvement completed in 1915. L. H. Local Consul, E. H. Harris.

12

Indiana

LA PORTE

N.Y. **S.F.** Pop. 16,000. Alt. 812 feet. County seat, LaPorte County.

814 **2517** Three hotels, 4 garages. Local speed limit 8-15 miles per hour, enforced. Route marked through city and county, signs at city limits. One railroad crossing at grade, 5 banks, 3 railroads, 90 general business places, 3 express **12** companies, 2 telephone companies, 2 newspapers, 8 public schools, electric lights, trolley and water works, about 30 factories. Commercial Club. L. H. Local Consul, Judge J. C. Richter.

WESTVILLE

N.Y. **S.F.** Pop. 560. Alt. 789 feet. LaPorte County.

826 **2505** One hotel, 2 garages. Local speed limit 15 miles per hour, enforced. Route marked through town and county, signs at town limits. One railroad crossing at grade, not **11** protected. One bank, 2 railroads, 27 general business places, 2 express companies, 2 telephone companies, 1 newspaper, 1 public school, electric lights.

VALPARAISO

N.Y. **S.F.** Pop. 6,987. Alt. 736 feet. County seat, Porter County.

837 **2494** Three hotels, 5 garages. State law governs local speed limit. Extensive road improvement completed in 1915. Three banks, 3 railroads, 1 interurban line, 2 express companies, 1 telephone company, 3 newspapers, 4 public schools, **8** electric lights and water works; Valparaiso University with an average enrollment of 3,500 students. L. H. Consul, Percy L. Sisson, Mayor. All road information at Wheeler-Elam Garage.

DEEP RIVER

N.Y. **S.F.** Pop. 60. Lake County.

845 **2486** No accommodations for tourists. Route marked through **7** town and county.

MERRILLVILLE

N.Y. **S.F.** Pop. 215. Lake County.

852 **2479** One hotel, 1 garage. Route marked through town and county. One railroad, 1 express company, 1 telephone **6** company. L. H. Local Consul, Walker Brothers.

Indiania

SCHERERVILLE

N.Y.	S.F.	Pop. 190. Lake County.
858	2473	No tourist accommodations. Local speed limit 8 miles per hour, enforced. Route marked through town and county, signs at town limits. Extensive road improvement completed in 1915. One railroad crossing at grade, not protected. One railroad, 1 express company.
	3	

DYER

N.Y.	S.F.	Pop. 500. Alt. 637 feet. Lake County.
861	2470	One hotel, 1 garage. Route marked through town and county, signs at town limits. One railroad crossing at grade, protected. One bank, 3 railroads, 20 general business places, 1 express company, 2 telephone companies, 2 public schools, electric lights. Commercial Club.
	8	

DYER to JOLIET, ILLINOIS

This section of the Lincoln Highway is mostly gravelled and in good condition with the exception of about 3 miles.

—, "*it is obvious that this Association can only aid and co-operate toward the desired end, and that UPON ALL THE PEOPLE, and especially upon the officials of each State and County and upon the inhabitants thereof, within the borders' of which is designated by these resolutions, a section of the Lincoln Highway, does rest the patriotic burden of establishing, broadening, straightening, maintaining and beautifying such Highway to the end that it may become an appropriate memorial to the Great Martyred Patriot whose name it bears.*"

—From the Proclamation of the Route of the
Lincoln Highway, Issued Sept. 13th, 1913.

An Appeal for Financial Aid

The Lincoln Highway Association appeals to every patriotic American for financial aid in degree commensurate with his means. As a national project of the greatest public value it deserves and justifies this support. Nowhere could funds be better invested for the present and future gain of the nation as a whole. Good roads mean progress, prosperity and pleasure; our future advancement will be along the line of our permanent roads. The Lincoln Highway typifies in the public mind the good roads movement in this country today. As it progresses toward the ultimate completion, so the thousands of miles of connecting roads and interconnecting branches progress.

Because of nation-wide co-operation great things have been accomplished at very small expense. A very few have so far borne the major part of the burden but a constant support widespread in its origin has made up the necessary balance.

Methods of Contribution

Founders

The contribution of the sum of $1,000.00 or more, constitutes the donor a Founder of the Lincoln Highway Association, and places his name among those of the public-spirited patriots who will undoubtedly go down in history as national benefactors in the fostering of the work. To Americans of success and wealth from whom such support is possible, the Lincoln Highway Association particularly appeals. In the plans for financing the work of the Association, twenty-five Founders a year are needed, and more are exceedingly desirable.

Member Contributors

The Association appeals to those hundreds of thousands of interested and approving friends in every section of the United States, who cannot, no matter how great their desire, contribute such a substantial sum to the work. At least five dollars once is every man's share, and if every man, if every motorist even, did his share the Lincoln Highway would be built in a year.

Become a member of the Association by contributing five dollars or more. Every contributor receives a membership card in the Association and a radiator emblem for the automobile.

Illinois

L. H. STATE CONSUL, J. W. CORKINGS,
De Kalb, Illinois

L. H. CHICAGO CONSUL, WM G. EDENS,
Central Trust Co. of Ill., Chicago, Ill.

GENERAL INFORMATION

TOURISTS will find that gravel roads predominate in this State but a growing sentiment towards cement construction exists. Future building of that material seems assured. There is one "seedling mile" in Whiteside County and one in De Kalb, the latter being the first in the United States, the cement for the construction of both being contributed by the Lincoln Highway Association. A number of other such miles are to be built. About $407,500.00 have so far been spent in improving the Lincoln Highway through Illinois and, as the highway is a state aid road, the state has contributed $76,000.00 of this amount.

The Illinois law regulating the speed of automobiles is similar to that of Indiana, holding that 10, 15 and 25 miles per hour to be the greatest speeds allowable when a motor vehicle is reasonably and prudently driven.

LOOK FOR L. H. SIGN AND TURN TO RIGHT TO CHICAGO HEIGHTS

CHICAGO HEIGHTS

N.Y. 869   **S.F. 2462**   Pop. 20,000. Cook County.
Two hotels, 7 garages. Local speed limit, 15 miles per hour, enforced. Route marked through city and county, signs at city limits. Two railroad crossings at grade, protected. Three banks, 4 railroads, 400 general business places, 2 express companies, 2 telephone companies, 2 newspapers, 16 public schools, paved streets, electric lights, trolley and water works. Automobile Club. L. H. Local Consul, Ralph E. McEldowney.

24

JOLIET

N.Y. 893   **S.F. 2438**   Pop. 36,934. County seat, Will County. On the Des Plaines River.
Four hotels, including new $250,000 structure, price $1.00 up, 6 garages. Local speed limit 10-15 miles per hour.

Illinois

10 Route marked through city and county, signs at city limits. Four banks, 6 railroads, about 150 general business places, 4 express companies, 2 telephone companies, 1 newspaper, 28 public schools, electric lights, trolley, water works. Commercial Club. · The state penitentiary is located here. Public library, 2 hospitals, a club house for working men, $250,000 high school building, steel plants, stove and boiler works, machine shops, agricultural implement works, engine, match, box, pottery, brick and chemical factories, etc. Several of the largest limestone quarries in the United States are found here.

JOLIET to GENEVA

This section of the route of the Lincoln Highway is mainly concrete with some macadam.

PLAINFIELD

N.Y. **S.F.** Pop. 1,019. Will County.

903 **2428** One hotel, 3 garages. Local speed limit 15 miles per hour. Route marked through city and county. Extensive road improvement completed in 1915. One railroad crossing at grade, not protected. One bank, 3 railroads, 30 gen-

14 eral business places, 1 express company, 2 telephone companies, 1 newspaper, 1 public school, electric lights and water works. Commercial Club. L. H. County Consul, U. S. G. Blakeley.

AURORA

N.Y. **S.F.** Pop. 33,222. Alt. 648 feet.' Kane County.

917 **2414** Six hotels, 10 garages. Local speed limit 10-15 miles per hour, enforced. Route marked through city and county, signs at city limits. Extensive road improvement completed in 1915. One railroad crossing at grade, protected.

5 Seven banks, 4 railroads, 285 general business places, 3 express companies, 2 telephone companies, 1 newspaper, 19 public schools, electric lights, trolley and water works. Commercial Club, Automobile Club. L. H. Local Consul, Robert C. Horr; County Consul, M. K. Guyton.

MOOSEHEART

N.Y. **S.F.** Kane County.

922 **2409** No tourist accommodations. One garage. Route marked through town and county. 1 express company, 1 public school. Headquarters of the Loyal Order of Moose of the World, $10,000,000.00 Vocational School and Home for dependent children now under construction. Visitors welcome.

4 First section of Lincoln Highway undertaken and completed in 1914. This is concrete, 16 feet wide. It was constructed and dedicated to public use by the Order of the Moose as their contribution to the Lincoln Highway. L. H. Local Consul, Rodney H. Brandon, Sec'y-Treas.

BATAVIA

N.Y. **S.F.** Pop. 5,000. Kane County.

926 **2405** Two hotels, $1.50, American plan, 2 garages. Local speed limit, 8 miles per hour, not enforced. Route marked

Illinois

3   through town and county. Two railroad crossings at grade, protected. Two banks, 2 railroads, 150 general business places, 1 express company, 1 telephone company, 1 newspaper, 6 public schools, electric lights, trolley, water works. Commercial Club. L. H. Local Consul, C. C. Collins.

GENEVA

N.Y.   S.F.   Pop. 3,500. Alt. 720 feet. County seat, Kane County.

929   2402   One hotel, 2 garages. Local speed limit 10 miles per hour, enforced. Route marked through town and county. Extensive road improvement planned for 1916. Four railroad crossings, protected. Two banks, 1 railroad, 1 **25**   electric road, 50 general business places, 2 express companies, 1 telephone company, 1 newspaper, 3 public schools, electric lights, trolley and water works. Commercial Club. L. H. Local Consul, Mr. McIntosh.

GENEVA TO DE KALB

Generally excellent gravel roads.

DE KALB

N.Y.   S.F.   Pop. 9,250. Alt. 886 feet. DeKalb County.

954   2377   Two hotels, $2.00, American plan, 5 garages. Local speed limit 10 miles per hour, enforced. Route marked through city and county, signs at city limits. Eight miles of concrete road radiates from this town on the Lincoln Highway. Two railroad crossings at grade, protected. Four banks, 3 railroads, 225 general business places, 3 express companies, 2 telephone companies, 3 newspapers, 5 public **5**   schools, electric lights, water works, 2 interurban lines. Commercial Club. L. H. State Consul, J. W. Corkings. L. H. County Consul, J. H. Jarboe.

This city was the first of a large number of cities, towns and villages along the Lincoln Highway to re-name its principal thoroughfare "Lincoln Highway." This was done through the activities of the State Consul, who resides here, assisted by the citizens of the community.

Illinois

DE KALB to MALTA

Oiled dirt road, maintained in fair condition. Near Malta the tourist will encounter a mile of concrete road. This was the first "seedling mile" constructed on the Lincoln Highway. It was completed and dedicated to the public in November, 1914.

MALTA

N.Y. **S.F.** Pop. 450. Alt. 915 feet. DeKalb County.

959 **2372** No tourist accommodations. Two garages. Local speed limit, 10 miles per hour, enforced. Route marked through town and county, signs at town limits. One railroad, 1 express company, 1 telephone company.

6 First "Seedling Mile" built of concrete, just west of town. Work began September, 1914, completed November, 1914. Cement contributed by the Lincoln Highway Association. Work done under supervision of J. W. Corkings, State Consul, of DeKalb, Ill.

CRESTON

N.Y. **S.F.** Pop. 354. Alt. 903 feet. Ogle County.

965 **2366** Two hotels, 2 garages. Route marked through town and county, signs at town limits. Road improvement completed in 1915. One bank, 1 railroad, 5 general business

6 places, 1 express company, 1 telephone company, 1 public school, water works. L. H. Local Consul, Martin Kennedy.

ROCHELLE

N.Y. **S.F.** Pop. 3,000. Alt. 802 feet. Ogle County.

971 **2360** Three hotels, 5 garages. Route marked through city and county, signs at city limits. One railroad crossing at grade, not protected. Three banks, 3 railroads, 100 general business places, 2 express companies, 1 telephone

11 company, 3 newspapers, 3 public schools, electric lights and water works. L. H. Local Consul, M. L. Pickle. County Consul, W. P. Graham.

ROCHELLE to ASHTON

There is some gravel and some stone roads—generally good.

ASHTON

N.Y. **S.F.** Pop. 850. Alt. 817 feet. Lee County.

982 **2349** Two hotels, 2 garages. Local speed limit 6 miles per hour, generally enforced. Route marked through town and county, signs at town limits. Some road improvement completed in 1915. Two banks, 1 railroad, about 50

5 general business places, 1 express company, 1 telephone company, 1 newspaper, 1 public school, gas and electric lights. L. H. Local Consul, Frank S. Hart.

ASHTON to FRANKLIN GROVE

Well maintained oiled dirt road.

Illinois

FRANKLIN GROVE

N.Y. **S.F.** Pop. 700. Alt. 810. Lee County.

987 **2344** Two hotels, 1 garage. Route marked through town and county. Road improved in 1915. One railroad crossing at grade, protected. One bank, 1 railroad, 40 general **5** business places, 1 express company, 1 telephone company, 1 newspaper, 1 public school, electric lights, water works. Local Consul, I. J. Trostle.

FRANKLIN GROVE to FULTON

This section of the Lincoln Highway is of dirt, gravel and concrete construction—generally well maintained and oiled.

NACHUSA

N.Y. **S.F.** Pop. 100. Lee County.

992 **2339** No tourist accommodations. Route marked through town and county. Extensive road improvement completed in **5** 1915. One express company, 1 telephone company. L. H. Local Consul, E. L. Crawford.

DIXON

N.Y. **S.F.** Pop. 10,000. Alt. 725 feet. County seat, Lee County.

997 **2334** Four hotels, 4 garages. Local speed limit 10-15 miles per hour, enforced. Route marked through city and county, signs at city limits. Extensive road improvement completed in 1915. One railroad crossing at grade. Three banks, 2 railroads, about 150 general business places, 1 express company, 1 telephone company, 4 newspapers, 7 public schools, electric lights, trolley and water works. Commercial Club. L. H. County Consul, Rev. A. B. Whitecomb.

13 Look up monument marking the scene of one of the joint debates between Abraham Lincoln and Stephen A. Douglas. See Lincoln Room in Nachusa Tavern.

Dixon, as a frontier post, owned and occupied by John Dixon, was the headquarters of the United States troops and militia during the Black Hawk war of 1813.

At this place, there were gathered at one time Abraham Lincoln, Captain of militia; Robert Anderson, of Fort Sumter fame; Lieut. Jefferson Davis, later President of the Southern Confederacy; Lieut. Col. Zachary Taylor, and Lieut. Albert Sidney Johnson. It should be noted that the two men most prominent in the Civil War were fighting side by side in the Black Hawk war in Illinois and were living together in the one building composing the outpost, Fort Dixon.

Fort Dixon was built on the north bank of the river, just west of the Lincoln Highway.

STERLING

N.Y. **S.F.** Pop. 7,467. Alt. 648 feet. Whiteside County. On the Rock River at the head of the Illinois-Mississippi Canal.

1010 **2321** Three hotels, 3 garages. Local speed limit 12 miles per hour, enforced. Route marked through city and county, **15** signs at city limits. Four banks, 2 railroads, 150 general

Illinois

business places, 2 express companies, 1 telephone company, 2 newspapers, 7 public schools, electric lights, trolley and water works, good fishing. Commercial Club. L. H. Local Consul, W. F. Miller.

"Seedling Mile" completed on Lincoln Highway west of city.

One of the standard Lincoln Highway seedling miles will be traveled just west of Sterling. This mile built with concrete furnished by the Lincoln Highway Association is one of the factors responsible for the strong sentiment now existing for further similar improvement on the Lincoln Highway in this vicinity.

STERLING to FULTON

Between these two points the road is of concrete and brick completed in fall of 1915, and is now all in good shape except about 3½ miles of dirt.

MORRISON

N.Y.   **S.F.**   Pop. 3,000.   County seat, Whiteside County.

1025   **2306**   Three hotels, 2 garages. Local speed limit 15 miles per hour, not enforced. Route marked through town and county, signs at town limits. Road improved in 1915, concrete, 16 feet. Three banks, 1 railroad, about 100 general business places, 1 express company, 1 telephone company, 1 newspaper, 2 public schools, electric lights, water works. Commercial Club. Morrison is 12 miles from the Mississippi River. L. H. County Consul, Edward A. Smith.

14

FULTON

N.Y.   **S.F.**   Pop. 2,174. Alt. 594 feet. Whiteside County, on the Mis-

1039   **2292**   sissippi River.

Two hotels, 3 garages. State law governs local speed limit, enforced. Three railroad crossings at grade, protected. Concrete and brick improvements, 1915. Toll bridge across Mississippi River, 15c per car, 5c per passenger. Two banks, 2 railroads, 50-60 general business places, 3 express companies, 1 telegraph company, 1 newspaper, 2 public schools, electric lights and water works. L. H. Local Consul, M. W. Ingwerson, Mayor.

2

The Lincoln Highway crosses the Mississippi River at Fulton, Illinois, into Clinton, Iowa, there being two highway bridges, one at the north end of the city, the other at the south end of the city, both open night and day. Lincoln Highway markers will direct tourists to the approaches of both bridges on the Iowa and Illinois sides.

Iowa

L. H. STATE CONSUL, W. F. COAN,
Clinton, Iowa

GENERAL INFORMATION:

THE Lincoln Highway tourist crossing the State of Iowa will travel through one of the richest rural communities in the world. At the present time, an unfortunate legislative enactment prohibits the anticipation of public revenue for the construction of hard-surfaced roadways by bond issue. However, the highway laws of the State will undoubtedly be amended at the next session of the Legislature so that such improvements may be made, as the sentiment of the people demands it. The press of the State, the Lincoln Highway Consuls and various civic and Grange organizations are united in demanding the construction of hard-surfaced roads. The people of the State of Iowa have done everything in their power to bring the Lincoln Highway up to the highest standard of improved road. In the past two years, $247,000.00 have been spent for grading and bridge building along the route. $150,000.00 more have been spent in graveling the road. The Lincoln Highway gets constant attention. It now almost equals a railroad grade clear across the State and is ready for hard-surfacing as soon as legislative enactment will permit. No doubt exists of the willingness of the people in the counties through which the Lincoln Highway runs to bond themselves for this purpose.

The laws of Iowa hold that a motor vehicle must be so driven in a careful and prudent manner as not to endanger the property of another or the life and limb of any person. A speed in excess of 25 miles an hour is presumptive evidence that an automobile is not being so driven.

The tourist crosses the Mississippi River between Fulton and Clinton, where brick pavement is encoutered through the city.

Iowa

CLINTON

N.Y.   **S.F.**   Pop. 27,000. Alt. 589 feet. County seat, Clinton County,
1041   **2290**   midway between Chicago and Omaha. On the Mississippi River.

10

Five hotels, 5 garages. Local speed limit 15 miles per hour, enforced. Route marked through city and county, signs at city limits. Extensive road improvement completed in 1915. One railroad crossing at grade, protected. Two toll bridges over the Mississippi, 15c per car, 5c per passenger. Eight banks, 5 railroads, 250 general business places, 100 factories, 4 express companies, 2 telephone companies, 5 newspapers, 24 public schools, public buildings and parks, $100,000 coliseum, convention hall and armory. Furniture, lumber, sugar refining, bridge works, harness, paper mills, flour mills, wire cloth. Chapter of nearly every national order, Commercial Club. L. H. State Consul, W. F. Coan. Local Consul, J. Q. Jeffries.

Here the tourist may detour from the Lincoln Highway north over a good road to Dubuque, from there if desired, continuing north along the western shore of the Mississippi River over a route, the construction of which is being promoted by the cities of McGregor, Dubuque and Clinton, and which will be known as the Eastern Iowa Scenic Route. The tourist can also, if desired, turn south at Clinton over a continuation of the Eastern Iowa Scenic Route leading to Daven-

Iowa

port on the Mississippi and along the western shore of that river, through Burlington, to the southern state line. This drive is said to be one of the most beautiful in the state, and enables the tourist to see the Tri-Cities of Davenport, Moline and Rock Island on the Mississippi, and the Government Arsenal Island, returning from the southern trip over a good road indicated on the map in blue, connecting Davenport with DeWitt on the Lincoln Highway, a 20 mile run directly north.

ELVIRA

N.Y.   **S.F.**   Pop. 31. Clinton County.

1051   **2280**   Route marked through town and county, signs at approach to town. Extensive road improvement completed in 1915.

12

DE WITT

N.Y.   **S.F.**   Pop. 1,875. Alt. 711 feet. Clinton County.

1063   **2268**   Two hotels, 5 garages. Local speed limit 12 miles per hour, not enforced. Route marked through town and county, signs at town limits. Extensive road improvement planned for 1916. One railroad crossing at grade, not protected. Three banks, 2 railroads, 40 general business places, 2 express companies, 1 telephone company, 1 newspaper, 2 public schools, electric lights and water works. Crystal Lake 2½ miles west, good fishing and camp site. Commercial Club. L. H. County Consul, A. M. Price.

5

GRAND MOUND

N.Y.   **S.F.**   Pop. 500. Alt. 721 feet. Clinton county.

1068   **2263**   One hotel, one garage. Local speed limit 10 miles per hour, enforced. Route marked through village and county, signs at village limits. One railroad crossing at grade, protected by bells. Two banks, 1 railroad, 25 general business places, 1 express company, 1 telephone company, 1 public school, Commercial Club. L. H. Consul, Julius Rheiman.

6

CALAMUS

N.Y.   **S.F.**   Pop. 270. Clinton County.

1074   **2257**   One hotel, 1 garage. Local speed limit 10 miles per hour enforced. Route marked through town and county. Extensive road improvement planned for 1916. One express company, 1 telephone company.

4

WHEATLAND

N.Y.   **S.F.**   Pop. 500. Alt. 683 feet. Clinton County.

1078   **2253**   Two hotels, two garages. Local speed limit 15 miles per hour, enforced. Route marked through village and county, signs at village limits. Two banks, 2 railroads, 30 general business places, 2 express companies, 1 telephone company, 1 newspaper, 1 public school, water works. L. H. Local Consul, Henry Guenther.

6

Iowa

LOWDEN

N.Y. **S.F.** Pop. 630. Alt. 717 feet Cedar County.

1084 **2247** Two hotels, one garage. Local speed limit 10 miles per hour, enforced. Route marked through village and county. Two banks, 1 railroad, 25 general business places, 1 express

9 company, 1 telephone company, 1 newspaper, 3 public schools. L. H. Local Consul, Dr. H. A. Runkel.

CLARENCE

N.Y. **S.F.** Pop. 700. Alt. 825 feet. Cedar County.

1093 **2238** One hotel, three garages. Local speed limit 10 miles per hour, enforced. Route marked through town and county, signs at town limits. Extensive road improvement planned for 1916. Two banks, 1 railroad, 32 general business places,

5 1 express company, 1 telephone company, 1 newspaper, 1 public school, electric lights, water works. Commercial Club, Automobile Club. L. H. County Consul, R. O. Hoyer.

STANWOOD

N.Y. **S.F.** (One-quarter mile north of Lincoln Highway. Continue straight ahead unless supplies are needed.)

1098 **2233** Pop. 500. Alt. 847 feet. Cedar County.

One hotel, 1 garage. Local speed limit 10 miles per hour,

5 enforced. One bank, 1 railroad, 14 general business places, 1 public school, 1 express company, 1 telephone company, 1 newspaper, electric lights, water works, Commercial Club. L. H. Local Consul, Homer Hart.

MECHANICSVILLE

N.Y. **S.F.** Pop. 875. Cedar County.

1103 **2228** Two hotels, 2 garages. Local speed limit 10 miles per hour, not enforced. Route marked through town and county. Extensive road improvement planned for 1916. Two banks, 1 railroad, 25 general business places, 1 express

7 company, 1 telephone company, 1 newspaper, 1 public school, electric lights, water works. L. H. Local Consul, O. M. Bundy.

Iowa

LISBON

N.Y. **S.F.** Pop. 846. Linn County.

1110 **2221** Two hotels, one garage. Local speed limit, 15 miles per hour, not enforced. Route marked through county, signs at town limits. One railroad, 2 express companies, 2 telephone companies, 2 banks. Rich agricultural district.

2

MT. VERNON

N.Y. **S.F.** Pop. 1,800. Alt. 843 feet. Linn County.

1112 **2219** Two hotels, 2 garages. Local speed limit 10 miles per hour, enforced. Route marked through town and county, signs at town limits. Extensive road improvement planned for 1916. Two banks, 1 railroad, 50 general business places, 1 express company, 1 telephone company, 2 newspapers, 2 public schools, park, electric lights, trolley, water works. Commercial Club.

13

MARION

N.Y. **S.F.** Pop. 5,000. Alt. 850 feet. Linn County.

1125 **2206** Three hotels, 2 garages. Local speed limit 15 miles per hour, enforced. Route marked through city and county, signs at city limits. Extensive road improvement completed in 1915 and more planned for 1916. One railroad crossing at grade. Three banks, 1 railroad, 60 general business places, 1 express company, 1 telephone company, 2 newspapers, 4 public schools, electric lights, trolley and water works. Commercial Club. L. H. Local Consul, Edw. J. Otterbein.

5

CEDAR RAPIDS

N.Y. **S.F.** Pop. 42,000. Alt. 837 feet. Linn County.

1130 **2201** Eleven hotels, 12 garages. Local speed limit 15-20 miles per hour, enforced. Route marked through city and county, signs at city limits. Two railroad crossings at grade, protected. Ten banks, 4 railroads, 3 interurban lines, 2 express companies, 1 telephone company, 4 newspapers, 25 public schools, public play grounds and bathing beaches, natural scenic features, Elks' Home, 192 factories, largest cereal mills in the world, starch works, meat packing plant. Automobile Club, Commercial Club. L. H. County Consul, W. G. Haskell; Local Consul, J. D. Blue, Jr.

37

The distance from Cedar Rapids to Belle Plain is 37 miles, and if the tourist has been encountering bad weather it is extremely advisable to make inquiry in Cedar Rpaids as to road conditions before proceeding further. Heavy rains can easily make this portion of the Highway difficult to travel.

BELLE PLAINE

N.Y. **S.F.** Pop. 4,000. Alt. 824 feet. Benton County.

1167 **2164** Three hotels, three garages. Local speed limit, 12 miles per hour, enforced. Route marked through city and county. Three banks, 1 railroad, 75 general business places, 1 express company, 1 telephone company, 2 newspapers, 4 public schools, electric lights and water works. Commercial Club. L. H. County Consul, O. C. Burrows.

6

Iowa

CHELSEA

N.Y. **S.F.** Pop. 600. Alt. 789 feet. Tama County. On the Iowa
1173 **2158** River.

Two hotels, 1 garage. Local speed limit, 12 miles per hour, enforced. Route marked through town and county, signs at town limits. Two banks, 1 railroad, 11 general

7 business places, 1 express company, 2 telephone companies, electric lights and water works. Good fishing and good camp site.

GLADSTONE

N.Y. **S.F.** Pop. 50. Tama County.
1180 **2151** No tourist accommodations. One railroad, telegraph sta-

5 tion.

TAMA

N.Y. **S.F.** Pop. 2,500. Alt. 827 feet. Tama County. On the Iowa
1185 **2146** River.

Two hotels, 2 garages. Route marked through town and county. Two railroad crossings at grade. Two banks, 3 railroads, 50 general business places, 2 express companies, 1 telephone company, 2 newspapers, 2 public schools, electric lights, water works. Commercial Club. L. H.

8 County Consul, D. E. Goodell.

Three miles west of here the Highway passes directly through the Sac and Fox Indian Reservation, the only reservation on the Lincoln Highway east of the Missouri River.

The Indians settled here, coming from what is now Oklahoma, in 1855 and still cling to many of their habits as to dress and traditions.

MONTOUR

N.Y. **S.F.** Pop. 500. Tama County.
1193 **2138** One hotel, three garages. Local speed limit, 15 miles per hour, enforced. Route marked through town and county. One railroad crossing at grade, protected. One bank, 1

2 railroad, 15 general business places, 1 express company, 1 telephone company, 1 public school, electric lights.

Iowa

BUTLERVILLE

N.Y.   **S.F.**   Tama County. Post Office address "Montour".

1195   **2136**   No tourist accommodations. L. H. Local Consul, Frank Lewis.

2

LE GRAND

N.Y.   **S.F.**   Pop. 363. Alt. 933 feet. Marshall County.

1197   **2134**   Two hotels, 1 garage. Local speel limit, 10 miles per hour. Route marked through town and county, signs at town limits. One railroad crossing at grade, not protected. One bank, 1 railroad, 1 newspaper, 2 public schools, electric lights. Commercial Club. "Devil's Anvil", a huge rocky promontory, 1 mile east. Immense quarries and the largest stone crushing plant in the United States. L. H. Local Consuls, Corwin O'Neil, and E. L. Condon.

10

MARSHALLTOWN

N.Y.   **S.F.**   Pop. 16,029. County seat, Marshall County.

1207   **2124**   Six hotels, 6 garages. Local speed limit, 15 miles per hour, not enforced. Route marked through city and county. Lincoln Highway will be cement paved clear through the city in 1916. Five banks, 3 railroads, 400 general business places, 3 express companies, 2 telephone companies, 2 newspapers, 9 public schools, electric lights, trolley and water works. Commercial Club, Automobile Club. L. H. County Consul, A. A. Moore.

14
(To La Moille)

Indian Reservation, 16 miles east. Attention called to grade elimination west of city which involved the handling of many thousands of cubic yards of material by steam shovel.

STATE CENTER

(One-quarter mile east of Lincoln Highway. Continue straight ahead unless supplies are needed.)
Pop. 1,037. Exact center of state.

Two hotels, 5 garages, 2 banks, 2 express companies, 2 railroads. Local Consul, I. D. Kauffman.

Iowa

LA MOILLE

N.Y. **S.F.** Pop. 120. Alt. 931 feet. Marshall County.

1221 **2110** No accommodations for tourists. One garage. Route marked through county. Extensive road improvement planned for 1916. One railroad, 4 general business places, **9** 1 express company, 1 telephone company, 1 public school. L. H. Local Consul, S. W. Myers.

COLO

N.Y. **S.F.** Pop. 500. Alt. 1,038 feet. Story County.

1230 **2101** One hotel, 1 garage. Local speed limit 10 miles per hour, enforced. Route marked through town and county, signs at town limits. Two railroad crossings at grade, protected. Two banks, 1 railroad, 25 general business places, 1 ex- **7** press company, 1 telephone company, 1 newspaper, 1 public school. Masonic, O. E. S., Oddfellow, M. W. A. and M. W. W. lodges.

NEVADA

N.Y. **S.F.** Pop. 2,500. Alt. 996 feet. County Seat, Story County.

1237 **2094** Two hotels, 2 garages. Local speed limit 10 miles per hour, not enforced. Route marked through city and county. Three banks, 2 railroads, 94 general business places, 1 express company, 1 telephone company, 2 news- **8** papers, 4 public schools, electric lights, water works. Commercial Club, Automobile Club. L. H. Local Consul, E. T. Alderman.

AMES

N.Y. **S.F.** Pop. 5,067. Alt. 917 feet. Story County.

1245 **2086** Two hotels, 1 new, costing $250,000, 3 garages. Local speed limit 12-20 miles per hour, enforced. Two railroads, 1 express company, 6 banks, 1 telephone company. Iowa State College of Agriculture and Mechanical Arts located **2** here. Extensive buildings include an experimental station costing over $3,000,000.00. 14,000 acres of land used for experimental purposes. The L. H. here intersects Kansas City, Des Moines, Mason City and Twin City routes. L. H. County Consul, P. Sheldon.

Iowa

ONTARIO

N.Y. **S.F.** Pop. 125. Alt. 996 feet. Story County.

1247 **2084** One hotel, 1 garage. Route marked through county. One
general business place, 1 express company, 1 telephone
8 company, 1 public school.

JORDAN

N.Y. **S.F.** Pop. 25. Boone County.

1255 **2076** No tourist accommodations. One railroad, 1 express company, 1 telephone company.
6

BOONE

N.Y. **S.F.** Pop. 12,000. Alt. 1,134 feet. County seat, Boone County.

1261 **2070** Four hotels, 3 garages. Local speed limit 15 miles per
hour, enforced. Route marked through city and county.
Five banks, 3 railroads, 2 express companies, 1 telephone
company, 3 newspapers, 6 public schools, electric lights,
10 trolley and water works. Commercial Club, Automobile
Club. L. H. County Consul, J. L. Stevens. Local Consul,
S. G. Goldthwaite.

Boone is situated near the Des Moines River which, at
this point, passes through a narrow gorge. The country is
broken and picturesque and the hills are heavily tim-
bered on both sides of the river. The scenery pro-
duces a restful change on the traveler after many
miles of comparatively flat prairie east and west of
this point.

OGDEN

N.Y. **S.F.** Pop. 1,600. Alt. 1,087 feet. Boone County.

1271 **2060** One hotel, 2 garages. Local speed limit 10 miles per hour.
Route marked through town and county. One railroad
crossing at grade, dangerous, bad crossing, not protected.
Four banks, 3 railroads, 18 general business places, 2
11 express companies, 1 telephone company, 1 newspaper, 2
public schools, electric lights, trolley and water works.
Commercial Club.

GRAND JUNCTION

N.Y. **S.F.** Pop. 1,012. Alt. 1,036 feet. Greene County.

1282 **2049** Three hotels, 2 garages. Local speed limit 12 miles per
hour, enforced. Route marked through town and county,
signs at town limits. The route of the L. H. across
Greene County is being gravelled, the most of the work to
9 be completed in 1916. Two railroad crossings at grade,
protected. Two banks, 2 railroads, 2 express companies,
2 telephone companies, 1 newspaper, electric lights. Commercial Club.

JEFFERSON

N.Y. **S.F.** Pop. 3,000. Alt. 1,052 feet. County Seat, Greene County.

1291 **2040** Two hotels, 5 garages. Local speed limit 15 miles per
hour, enforced. Route marked through city and county.
9 Five banks, 2 railroads, 45 general business places, 2 express companies, 1 telephone company, 2 newspapers, 2

Iowa

public schools, electric lights and water works. Commercial Club and Automobile Club. L. H. County Consul, E. B. Wilson. Local Consul, P. L. Cockerill.

Attention directed to the Head Memorial Bridge, the second memorial of this character to be built. Greene County is said to be the seed corn county of the world.

SCRANTON

N.Y. **S.F.** Pop. 900. Alt. 1,172 feet. Greene County.

1300 **2031** One hotel, 2 garages. Local speed limit 12 miles per hour, enforced. Route marked through town and county, signs at town limits. One railroad crossing at grade, protected. Three banks, 1 railroad, 15 general business **6** places, 1 express company, 1 telephone company, 1 newspaper, 1 public school, electric lights and water works. Commercial Club.

RALSTON

N.Y. **S.F.** Pop. 200. Carroll County.

1306 **2025** One hotel, 1 garage. Local speed limit 10 miles per hour, enforced. Route marked through county. Extensive road improvement completed in 1915. One bank, 1 railroad, 3 **5** general business places, 1 express company, 1 telephone company, 1 public school, electric lights.

GLIDDEN

N.Y. **S.F.** Pop. 850. Alt. 1,221 feet. Carroll County.

1311 **2020** One hotel, 3 garages. Local speed limit 15 miles per hour, enforced. Route marked through town and county, **8** signs at town limits. One railroad, 1 express company, 1 telephone company.

CARROLL

N.Y. **S.F.** Pop. 4,000. County seat, Carroll County.

1319 **2012** Five hotels, 4 garages. Route marked through city and county, signs at city limits. One railroad crossing at grade. Four banks, 2 railroads, 2 general business places, **13** 2 express companies, 2 telephone companies, 3 newspapers, 5 public schools, electric lights, water works. Commercial Club. Carroll is an important trading center of a farming region. L. H. County Consul, W. B. Swaney.

Iowa

WEST SIDE

N.Y. **S.F.** Pop. 500. Alt. 1,321 feet. Crawford County.
1332 **1999** One hotel, 1 garage. Route marked through town and county, signs at town limits. Two banks, 1 railroad, 1 express company, 1 telephone company, 25 general business places, 1 newspaper, 1 public school, electric lights, water works.

6

VAIL

N.Y. **S.F.** Pop. 631. Alt. 1,255 feet. Crawford County.
1338 **1993** One hotel, 2 garages. Local speed limit 10 miles per hour, enforced. Route marked through town and county. One railroad, 1 express company, 1 telephone company.

10

DENISON

N.Y. **S.F.** Pop. 3,500. Alt. 1,171 feet. County seat, Crawford
1348 **1983** County.
Five hotels, 4 garages. Local speed limit 10 miles per hour, enforced. Route marked through city and county. One railroad crossing at grade, protected. Three banks, 2 railroads, 60 general business places, 1 express company,
8 1 telephone company, 3 newspapers, 3 public schools, electric lights and water works. Commercial Club. L. H. County Consul, G. L. Caswell. Local Consul, W. C. Rollins.

ARION

N.Y. **S.F.** Pop. 300. Alt. 1,149 feet. Crawford County.
1356 **1975** Two hotels, 1 garage. Local speed limit 10 miles per hour, enforced. Route marked through town and county, signs at town limits. Extensive road improvement planned for
2 1916. One bank, 3 railroads, 8 general business places, 2 express companies, 1. telephone company, 1 public school.

DOW CITY

N.Y. **S.F.** Pop. 700. Alt. 1,142 feet. Crawford County.
1358 **1973** One hotel, 2 garages. Route marked through town and county, signs at town limits. Extensive road improvement planned for 1916. One bank, 2 railroads, 26 general
9 business places, 1 express company, 1 telephone company, 1 newspaper, 1 public school, park, electric lights, water works.

DUNLAP

N.Y. **S.F.** Pop. 1,500. Alt. 1,092 feet. Harrison County.
1367 **1964** Two hotels, 2 garages. Local speed limit 10-15 miles per hour. Route marked through town and county, signs at town limits. Three banks, 2 railroads, 40 general business
12 places, 2 express companies, 2 telephone companies, 1 newspaper, 3 public schools, electric lights and water works. Commercial Club.

*The Sign of Superior
Motor Car Service*

Watch for This Good-Service Sign

Whether you drive a Hupmobile or not you will find under the blue and white sign, pictured above, service to your liking.

Only the best equipped garages and repair shops available in a community can secure a Hupmobile Service Representative's contract.

We train their mechanics to take care of Hupmobiles and it follows that they are more efficient men for the owner of any make of car to employ.

What Is Hupmobile Coupon Service?

Every buyer of a Series "N" Hupmobile receives a leather-bound book of coupons, good for 50 hours of labor in install-ments to suit your needs at any of the 4000 Hupmobile service stations.

This service is entirely free to the owner, and means that the car is kept in perfect running condition by Hupmobile experts.

Hupmobile service stations have been established, not only along the Lincoln Highway, but everywhere, expressly to render this free service to our owners.

This is the first national system of free service put into effect by any automobile manufacturer.

It is so complete, and means so much genuine satisfaction to the owner, that you should learn all its details.

Write for information, and for the Hupmobile Touring Guide —a book you will be glad to look over.

Hupp Motor Car Corporation
Detroit, Michigan

Iowa

WOODBINE

N.Y. **S.F.** Pop. 1,600. Alt. 1,053 feet. Harrison County.

1379 **1952** One hotel, 3 garages. Local speed limit 10 miles per hour, enforced. Route marked through town and county. Extensive road improvement planned for 1916. Two railroad crossings at grade, protected by bells. Two banks, 2 railroads, 57 general business places, 1 express company, 1 telephone company, 1 newspaper, 2 public schools, water works. Commercial Club. L. H. Local Consul, Lewis Haas.

10

LOGAN

N.Y. **S.F.** Pop. 1,500. Alt. 928 feet. County seat, Harrison County.

1389 **1942** One hotel, 3 garages. Route marked through town and county, signs at town limits. One railroad crossing at grade, not protected. Three banks, 2 railroads, 70 general business places, 1 express company, 1 telephone company, 2 newspapers, 1 public school, electric lights, water works. Commercial Club. L. H. County Consul, D. H. Seabury. Local Consul, Almor Stern.

7

MISSOURI VALLEY

N.Y. **S.F.** Pop. 4,000. Alt. 1,001 feet. Harrison County.

1396 **1935** Two hotels, 2 garages. Local speed limit 10-15 miles per hour, enforced. Route marked through town and county, signs at town limits. One railroad crossing at grade, protected. Three banks, 3 railroads, 75 general business places, 1 express company, 1 telephone company, 2 newspapers, 3 public schools, electric lights and water works. Commercial Club. L. H. Local Consul, R. D. McEvoy.

5

LOVELAND

N.Y. **S.F.** Pop. 100. Pottawattamie County.

1401 **1930** One hotel, no garage. Gas and oil to be obtained at hotel. Local speed limit 15 miles per hour, enforced. Route marked through town and county. One express company, 1 telephone company.

5

HONEY CREEK

N.Y. **S.F.** Pop. 100. Pottawattamie County.

1406 **1925** No hotel; boarding house, 1 garage. Route marked through town and county. Extensive road improvement completed in 1915.

5

CRESCENT

N.Y. **S.F.** Pop. 300. Alt. 990 feet. Pottawattamie County.

1411 **1920** Two hotels, 1 garage. Route marked through town and county, signs at town limits. One railroad, 5 general business places, 1 express company, 1 telephone company, 1 public school.

7

Iowa

COUNCIL BLUFFS

N.Y. **S.F.**
1418 **1913**

5

Pop. 30,778. County seat, Pottawattamie County. On the Missouri River.

Five hotels, 5 garages. Local speed limit 12 miles per hour, enforced. Route marked through city and county. Extensive road improvement completed in 1915 and more contemplated in 1916. $100,000.00 to be spent on Lincoln Highway within city limits. Bridge over Missouri River, 15c per car, 5c per passenger. Eight railroads, 4 express companies, 2 telephone companies, paved streets, parks, State Institution for the deaf, large public library, 8 large grain elevators. A beautiful summer resort 3 miles south of the city. Here, in 1846, the mormons established a settlement, called "Kanesville," which they soon abandoned for Salt Lake City. L. H. County Consul, Dr. Donald Macrea.

Between Council Bluffs and Omaha the tourist crosses the Missouri River over a fine steel bridge and enters Nebraska.

Nebraska

STATE CONSUL OF NEBRASKA, GEO. F. WOLTZ,
Mayor of Fremont

GENERAL INFORMATION

I N THIS state, the tourist will find many indications that assure the complete future improvement of this section of the Lincoln Highway. Two standard seedling miles are now finished, one at Grand Island and one at Kearney, and a considerable number more in addition are to be built in the immediate future. In Nebraska, the tourist will encounter many roads in varying degrees of excellence depending entirely upon the weather. The roads are generally maintained by dragging. Between Omaha and Kearney, frequent crossings of the Union Pacific Railroad are encountered and tourists are cautioned to use extreme care, although normally trains can be seen at long distances before the approach. In the past two years, over $100,000 has been spent in grading the Nebraska section of the Lincoln Highway. $60,000 has been spent for bridges and $30,000 has been spent in graveling this section of the route.

Nebraska

The Nebraska law applying to the speed of motor vehicles states that no such vehicle shall be operated on any highway at a rate of speed greater than that is reasonable and proper with 25 miles an hour as a maximum, and 12 miles an hour within any city or village.

OMAHA

N.Y. S.F.
1423 1908

16

Pop. 185,000. Alt. 1,030 feet. County seat, Douglas County. On the Missouri River. Eight hotels, including 1 new one costing $1,500,000., 10 garages. Local speed limit 12-20 miles per hour, enforced. Route marked through city and county. One railroad crossing at grade protected. One toll gate entering Omaha. One toll bridge, 15c, 10c and 5c. Nine banks, 8 railroads, 4 express companies, 1 telephone company, 5 newspapers, 45 public schools, electric lights, trolley and water works. Commercial Club, Automobile Club. L. H. County Consul, Harry Lawrie.

ELKHORN

N.Y. S.F.
1439 1892

4

Pop. 291. Alt. 1,165 feet. Douglas County. One hotel, 3 garages. Local speed limit 12 miles per hour, enforced. Route marked through town and county; signs at town limits. One railroad crossing at grade. Two banks, 1 railroad, 25 general business places, 1 express company, 1 telephone company, 1 newspaper, 1 public school, electric lights, water works, Commercial Club. L. H. Local Consul, Julius Schuldt.

WATERLOO

N.Y. S.F.
1443 1888

3

Pop. 500. Douglas County. No tourist accommodations. Route marked through town and county. One bank, 1 railroad, 1 express company, 2 telephone companies, 1 newspaper, 1 public school. Commercial Club. Electric lights. L. H. Local Consul, J. C. Robinson.

VALLEY

N.Y. S.F.
1446 1885

12

Pop. 900. Alt. 1,144 feet. Douglas County. Three hotels, 1 garage. Local speed limit 12 miles per hour, enforced. Route marked through town and county, signs at town limits. One bank, 1 railroad, 35 general business places, 1 express company, 1 telephone company, 1 newspaper, 2 public schools, Automobile Club, Commercial Club. L. H. Local Consul, W. G. Whitmore.

Nebraska

FREMONT

N.Y. **S.F.** Pop. 10,000. Alt. 1,198 feet. County seat, Dodge County.
1458 **1873** Four hotels, including a new one costing $200,000, 8 garages. Local speed limit 12 miles per hour, not enforced. Route marked through town and county. On Union Pacific, and Chicago and Northwestern railroads, Chicago, Burlington & Quincy railroad. Important grain market.

7 Seven banks, 3 railroads 125 general business places, 2 express companies, 2 telephone companies, 3 newspapers, 10 public schools, paved streets, electric lights and water works. Commercial Club, Automobile Club. L. H. State Consul, George Wolz; Local Consul, Otto Schurman.

Nebraska

AMES

N.Y. **S.F.** Pop. 24. Dodge County.

1465 **1866** No, tourist accommodations. Route marked through village and county, signs at approach of village. One railroad, 1 express company, 1 telephone company, L. H. Local Consul, Nat Johnson.

9

NORTH BEND

N.Y. **S.F.** Pop. 1,300. Alt. 1,274 feet. Dodge County.

1474 **1857** One hotel, 2 garages. Local speed limit 12 miles per hour. Route marked through town and county; signs at town limits. Extensive road improvement completed in 1915. Two banks, 1 railroad, 12 general business places, 1 express company, 1 telephone company, 1 newspaper, 1 public school, water works. Commercial Club. L. H. County Consul, Ray Cusack.

7

ROGERS

N.Y. **S.F.** Pop. 200. ColfaxCounty. On the Platte River.

1481 **1850** One hotel. Route marked through town and county. One bank, 1 railroad, 5 general business places, 1 express company, 1 telephone company, 1 public school. L. H. Consul, F. J. Henry.

8

SCHUYLER

N.Y. **S.F.** Pop. 3,000. Alt. 1,351 feet. County seat, Colfax County.

1489 **1842** Four hotels, three first class cafes, 4 garages. Local speed limit 10 miles per hour, enforced. Route marked through town and county, signs at town limits. Extensive road improvement planned for 1916. Largest exclusive hard wheat mill in world. One railroad crossing at grade, not protected. Three banks, 2 railroads, about 65 general busines places, 2 express companies, 2 telephone companies, 2 newspapers, 3 public schools, electric lights and water works. Commercial Club, Automobile Club. L. H. County Consul, J. E. McNally, Local Consuls, D. S. Conrad, J. Kopac.

8

Nebraska

RICHLAND P. O.

N.Y. **S.F.**
1497 **1834**

8

Pop. 156. Colfax County.
No tourist accommodations.
Local speed limit 10 miles per hour, enforced. Route marked through town and county; signs at town limits. Extensive road improvement planned for 1916. One railroad, 1 express company, 1 telephone company. L. H. Consul, G. A. Shonka.

COLUMBUS

N.Y. **S.F.**
1505 **1826**

9

Pop. 6,000. Alt. 1,448 feet. County seat, Platte County. Junction of Platte and Loup Rivers.
Four hotels, 5 garages. Local speed limit 10 miles per hour, enforced. Route marked through city and county. Extensive road improvement completed in 1915. One railroad crossing at grade, protected. Four banks, 2 railroads, 160 general business places, 2 express companies, 2 telephone companies, 3 newspapers, 5 public schools, public buildings and park, electric lights, water works. Commercial Club. L. H. County Consul, Henry Ragatz,
Through this city runs the Meridian Road from Winnipeg to the Gulf of Mexico.
Leaving Columbus, the Union Pacific R. R. track is absolutely straight for 40 miles across the prairie.
Coronado visited this locality in 1542 and found here large bodies of Indians. At the time of the early American explorers, the Loup Indians had a large settlement here and it was one of the principal council headquarters of the Indians of the Plains.

DUNCAN

N.Y. **S.F.**
1514 **1817**

9

Pop. 218. Alt. 1,495 feet. Platte County.
One hotel. One garage. Local speed limit 8 miles per hour, enforced. Route marked through town and county; signs at town limits. One bank, 1 railroad, 10 general business places, 1 express company. 1 telephone company, 1 newspaper, 2 public schools, Commercial Club. L. H. Local Consul, John P. Sokol.

SILVER CREEK

N.Y. **S.F.**
1523 **1808**

12

Pop. 700. Alt. 1,550 feet. Merrick County. On the Platte River.
Two hotels, 3 garages. Local speed limit 8 miles per hour, enforced. Route marked through town and county. Extensive road improvement planned for 1916. Two banks, 2 railroads, 20 general business places, 1 express company, 1 telephone company, 1 newspaper, 1 public school, electric lights, water works, Commercial Club. L. H. Local Consul, P. H. Bell.
One mile west of Silver Creek, the Lincoln Highway passes through Wooster's Lover's Lane, a delightful bit of shady road, with the trees meeting overhead from both sides of the road.

CLARKS

N.Y. **S.F.**
1535 **1796**

11

Pop. 605. Alt. 1,623 feet. Merrick County. On the Platte River.
One hotel, 2 garages. Local speed limit 8 miles per hour. Route marked through town and county; signs at town limits. One railroad, 1 express company, 1 telephone company.

Nebraska

CENTRAL CITY

N.Y. **S.F.**
1546 **1785**

Special Warning

At Central City, local antagonistic influence has removed the official markers from the direct efficient Lincoln Highway route, which goes directly west from Central City, paralleling the Union Pacific on the south side to Chapman and on to Grand Island.

10

Pop. 3,000. Alt. 1,704 feet. County seat, Merrick County. On the Platte River.

Three hotels, 4 garages. Local speed limit 10 miles per hour, not enforced. Route marked through town and county. Three banks, 3 railroads, 50 general business places, 2 express companies, 2 telephone companies, 2 newspapers, 3 public schools, electric lights, water works, Commercial Club, Automobile Club.

One mile west and two miles south of the city, on the north side of the Platte River, where the Old California Trail was located, stands a large stone image of the "Lone Tree" mentioned so many times by explorers over the prairie as early as 1833. It stood within a few yards of the Lone Tree Stage Station, from which the town of Lone Tree—now Central City —took its name. This was a giant cotton-wood and was a prominent landmark on the old trail. The stone monument was erected in 1911 by the County, showing that the people of this country are just awakening to the importance and desirability of marking all of the historical spots for posterity, and none are more historic nor of more vital interest than those spots which are closely connected with the history of the development of the great West.

The first meeting held in the United States to ratify the Proclamation of the Lincoln Highway, was held at Central City October 3, 1913.

CHAPMAN

N.Y. **S.F.**
1556 **1775**

15

Pop. 250. Alt. 1,770 feet. Merrick County. One hotel, 1 garage. Local speed limit 10 miles per hour, not enforced. Route marked through village and county; signs at approach to village. One railroad crossing at grade, not protected. One bank, 1 railroad, 7 general business places, 1 express company, 2 telephone companies, 3 public schools. L. H. Local Consul, Herman H. Bease.

GRAND ISLAND

N.Y. **S.F.**
1571 **1760**
8

Pop. 14,000. Alt. 1,860 feet. County seat, Hall County. Five hotels, 7 garages, 1 telephone company. Local speed limit, 12 miles per hour, enforced. Route marked through city and county. Extensive road improvement completed

Nebraska

in 1915, including a seedling mile. Three banks, 4 railroads, 150 general business places, 2 express companies, 2 telephone companies, 3 newspapers, 9 public schools, parks, electric lights, water works. Commercial Club. Automobile Club. Second largest horse market in the world, handling 25,000 horses annually. Soldiers' and Sailors' Home. L. H. County Consul, F. W. Ashton.

On June 26, 1842, Fremont camped on the south side of the river near this end of the Island on his first expedition to the far west, having come up from what is now Kansas City.

ALDA

N.Y. **S.F.**
1579 **1752**
10

Pop. 250. Alt. 1,917 feet Hall County. One hotel, 1 garage. Route marked through **town and** county. One bank, 1 railroad, 4 general business places, 1 express company, 1 telephone company, 1 public school. L. H. Local Consul, Frank Denman.

WOOD RIVER

N.Y. **S.F.**
1589 **1742**
8

Pop. 898. Alt. 1,989 feet. Hall County. One hotel, 2 garages. Local speed limit, 8 miles per hour, enforced. Route marked through town and county. Two banks, 1 railroad, 15 general business places, 1 express company, 1 telephone company, 1 newspaper, 1 public school, electric lights, water works. Commercial Club. L. H. Local Consul, S. W. Wilson.

SHELTON

N.Y. **S.F.**
1597 **1734**
6

Pop. 1,100. Alt. 2,022 feet. Buffalo County. Two hotels, 1 garage. Local speed limit 8 miles per hour, enforced. Route marked through town and county, signs at town limits. Road improvement planned for 1916. Two banks, 2 railroads, 25 general business places, 1 express company, 2 telephone companies 1 newspaper, 1 public school, electric lights, water works. Commercial Club. L. H. Local Consul, O. H. Crumley.

GIBBON

N.Y. **S.F.**
1603 **1728**
13

Pop. 1,000. Alt. 2,062 feet. Buffalo County. One hotel, 1 garage. Route marked through town and county. One railroad crossing at grade, 2 banks, 2 railroads, 15 general business places, 1 express company, 2 telephone companies, 1 newspaper, 1 public school, electric lights, water works. Commercial Club.

Nebraska

KEARNEY

N.Y. **S.F.** Pop. 8,000. Alt. 2,145 feet. County seat, Buffalo County.

1616 **1715** Four hotels, 4 garages. Route marked through city and county; signs at city limits. Extensive road improvement completed in 1915, including seedling mile. Two railroad crossings at grade, not protected. Three banks, 4 railroads, 140 general business places, 2 express companies, 2 telephone companies 3 newspapers, 7 public schools, public buildings and parks, electric lights, water works. State Industrial School for Boys. The Western State Normal School with one thousand students enrolled. The Kearney Military Academy; State Hospital for tubercular patients; $125,000 Government Building; bridge across the Platte River 1 mile long. Commercial Club. Automobile Club. L. H. County Consul, W. F. Bailey, Local Consul, T. H. Bolte.

10

On June 27, 1842, Fremont camped on the south side of the Platte river opposite this point.

Large herds of buffalo were encountered by him through this section of the prairie and frequent alarms of Indians kept the exploring party constantly on the alert.

Just to the south-east of the city and on the other side of the river, the Old Salt Lake Trail comes in from the southeast on its way to the west.

Nebraska

ODESSA

N.Y.	S.F.	
1626	1705	Pop. 55. Buffalo County.
	7	No tourist accommodations. Railroad station, 1 express company, 1 telephone company.

ELM CREEK

N.Y.	S.F.	
1633	1698	Pop. 720. Alt. 2262 feet. Buffalo County.
	10	Two hotels, 1 garage, 2 banks. One railroad, 1 express company, 1 telephone company, L. H. Local Consul, E. L. Sutton.

OVERTON

N.Y.	S.F.	
1643	1688	Pop. 600. Alt. 2,321 feet. Dawson County.
	10	One hotel, 2 garages. Local speed limit, 12 miles per hour, enforced. Route marked through town and county, signs at town limits Two banks, 1 railroad, 28 general business places, 1 express company, 1 telephone company, 1 newspaper, 1 public school, electric lights. L. H. Local Consul, F. A. Lavery.

LEXINGTON

N.Y.	S.F.	
1653	1678	Pop. 3,000. Alt. 2,385 feet. County seat, Dawson County. Two hotels, 3 garages. Local speed limit, 12 miles per hour, enforced. Route marked through town and county. Three banks, 3 railroads, 25 general business places, 1

Nebraska

18 express company, 2 telephone companies, 2 newspapers, 4 public schools, electric lights, water works. Commercial Club. L. H. County Consul, J. W. Radcliffe; Local Consuls, W. H. Wisda, C. C. May.

COZAD

N.Y. S.F. Pop. 1,200. Alt. 2,496 feet. Dawson County.

1671 1660 One hotel, 2 garages. Local speed limit, 8 miles per hour, enforced. Route marked through town and county. Extensive road improvement planned for 1916. 2 banks, 1 railroad, 30 general business places, 1 express company, 1 telephone company, 1 newspaper, 1 public school, electric lights, water works. Commercial Club. L. H. Local Consul. W. H. Brown.

11

GOTHENBURG

N.Y. S.F. Pop. 1,730. Alt. 2,557 feet. Dawson County.

1682 1649 One hotel, 2 garages. Route marked through town and county; signs at town limits. Extensive road improvement planned for 1916. 1 railroad crossing at grade, not protected. Two banks, 1 railroad, 30 general business places, 1 express company, 2 telephone companies, 2 newspapers, 3 public schools, electric lights, water works. An artificial lake covering 100 acres adjoins the corporation limits of the city. L. H. Local Consul, E. A. Calling, County Commissioner.

12 Here the Lincoln Highway crosses the Platte River to the south side, and follows for a time the Old Salt Lake Trail and that of the Pony Express and Overland Stage Coach, as well as the paths of the early explorers, Fremont and the others.

From here to North Platte, where the Highway again crosses the river to the north, the country swarmed with buffalo and Indians in the days of 1840.

At present the Lincoln Highway is forced to turn south, crossing the North Platte River at Gothenburg and following along the south bank of the North Platte River until it again crosses the river into North Platte. As soon as the new $50,000 bridge over the North Platte River is completed just east of North Platte, the tourist will follow through Gothenburg, Brady and Maxwell along the north bank of the North Platte River which is the more direct route and which will eliminate 18 miles between Gothenburg and North Platte. The bridge will be open for traffic some time during the early summer of 1916. Inquire at Gothenburg as to the condition of the North route.

BRADY

N.Y. S.F. Pop. 150. No tourist accommodations. Telegraph, telephone, supplies, railroad station.

1694 1637

21

Nebraska

MAXWELL

N.Y. **S.F.** Pop. 300. Alt. 2,713 feet. Lincoln County.

1715 **1616** One hotel, 2 garages. Route marked through town and county. Road improved in 1915. One railroad crossing at grade, not protected. One bank, 1 railroad, 20 general business places, 1 express company, 1 telephone company, **15** 1 newspaper, 1 public school, electric lights. Commercial Club, Automobile Club. L. H. Local Consul, A. F. Nugent.

NORTH PLATTE

N.Y. **S.F.** Pop. 6,000. Alt. 2,795 feet. County seat, Lincoln County.

1730 **1601** Situated between the North and South Platte Rivers. Five hotels, including a new one costing $150,000. Three garages. Local speed limit 12 miles per hour, enforced. Route marked through city and county. Three banks, one **13** railroad, 200 general business places, 1 express company, 2 telephone companies, 2 newspapers, 4 public schools, Commercial Club. L. H. County Consul, A. B. Hoagland.

In 1842, Fremont forded the river here through the quicksands and camped upon the point of land on which now stands the city of North Platte.

HERSHEY

N.Y. **S.F.** Pop. 450. Lincoln County. On the South Platte River.

1743 **1588** Three hotels, 2 garages. Local speed limit 10 miles per hour, enforced. Route marked through town and county. Extensive road improvements planned for 1916. One **7** railroad crossing at grade, protected. One bank, 1 railroad, 24 general business places, 1 express company, 2 telephone companies, 1 newspaper. L. H. Local Consul, D. Leyboldt.

SUTHERLAND

N.Y. **S.F.** Pop. 500. Lincoln County. On the South Platte River.

1750 **1581** One hotel. Two garages. Local speed limit 12 miles per hour, enforced. Route marked through town and county; signs at town limits. Road improved in 1915. Two banks, **13** 1 railroad, 18 general business places, 1 express company, 1 telephone company, 1 newspaper. L. H. Local Consul, A. W. Hootson.

Nebraska

PAXTON

N.Y. **S.F.** Pop. 300. Keith County. On the South Platte River.

1763 **1568** Four hotels, 2 garages. Local speed limit 6 miles per hour, enforced. Route marked through town and county; signs at approach of town. One bank, 1 railroad, 4 general business places, 1 express company, 1 telephone company, 1 public school. L. H. Local Consul.

12 In marching from here along the banks of the South Platte, Fremont says that his party was surrounded by a vast herd of buffalo, extending two or three miles to the rear and as far as the eye could reach in front, leaving around the expedition as it advanced, an open space of two or three hundred yards.

ROSCOE

N.Y. **S.F.** Keith County. On the South Platte River. No tourist
1775 **1556** accommodations. Route marked through County. Two small stores, 1 railroad.

8

OGALLALA

N.Y. **S.F.** Pop. 800. Alt. 3,216 feet County seat, Keith County. On
1783 **1548** the South Platte River.

Three hotels, 2 garages. Local speed limit, 10 miles per hour, enforced. Route marked through town and county.
11 Two banks, 1 railroad, 19 general business places, 1 express company, 2 telephone companies, 1 newspaper, 1 public school, electric lights and water works. L. H. County Consul, J. W. Welpton.

BRULE

N.Y. **S.F.** Pop. 200. Keith County. On the South Platte River.

1794 **1537** Two hotels, 1 garage. Local speed limit 15 miles per hour, enforced. Route marked through town and county. Extensive road improvement completed in 1915. One bank,
5 1 railroad, 4 general business places, 1 express company, 1 telephone company, 1 public school. L. H. Local Consul, O. P. Kilgore.

MEGEATH

N.Y. **S.F.** Keith County. On the South Platte River.
1799 **1532** No tourist accommodations. Railroad station.

5

Special
Warning **BIG SPRINGS**

If the tour-
ist wishes to **N.Y.** **S.F.** Pop. 350. Alt. 3,366 feet. Deuel County.
go to Denver
the best way **1804** **1527** Three hotels, 2 garages. Local speed limit, 10 miles per
is to continue hour, not enforced. Route marked through town and
straight on county; signs at town limits. Extensive road improvement
over the Lin- completed in 1915. One bank, 1 railroad, 20 general busi-
coln Highway **20** ness places, 1 express company, 2 telephone companies. 1
to Cheyenne, public school.
Wyoming,
thence south
over Colo- The tourist wishing to follow the official Lincoln Highway
rado State
Highway. straight west through Cheyenne, Wyoming, should not be

Nebraska

diverted at this point by markers or signs indicating that the Lincoln Highway turns southwest here to Denver. To keep on directly west over the official route keep right hand road, following main travel over hill at the east entrance to Big Springs. Numerous markers have been placed here to mislead the tourist.

CHAPPELL

N.Y. **S.F.** Pop. 600. Alt. 3,696 feet. County seat, Deuel County.

1824 **1507** Two hotels, 2 restaurants. Local speed limit, 8 miles per hour, enforced. Route marked through town and county, signs at town limits. Extensive road improvement planned for 1916. Two banks, 1 railroad, 30 general business **20** places, 1 express company, 1 telephone company, 1 newspaper, 1 publc school, electric lights and water works. Commercial Club. L. H. County Consul J. R. Wertz; Local Consul, L. O. Pfeiffer.

LODGE POLE

N.Y. **S.F.** Pop. 400. Alt. 3,828 feet. Cheyenne County

1844 **1487** One hotel, 2 garages. One railroad crossing at grade protected by bells. One bank, 2 railroads, 17 general business places, 1 express company, 1 telephone company, 1 **7** newspaper, 1 public school, electric lights, water works, Commercial Club. Lodge Pole takes its name from Lodge-pole pine, used extensively by Indians and whites in the construction of dwellings. Beautiful park that is always accessible to tourists. Local Consul, A. B. Persinger.

SUNOL

N.Y. **S.F.** Cheyenne County.

1851 **1480** No tourist accommodations. Railroad station.

10

Nebraska

SIDNEY

N.Y. **S.F.**

1861 **1470**

19

Pop. 1,500. Alt. 4,090 feet. County seat Cheyenne County. Five hotels, 4 garages. Local speed limit 10 miles per hour, not enforced. Route marked through town and county. Two banks, 2 railroads, 50 general business places, 2 express companies, 1 telephone company 1 newspaper, 5 public schools, electric lights. Automobile Club. L. H. County Consul, J. L. McIntosh.

POTTER

N.Y. **S.F.**

1880 **1451**

8

Pop. 200. Alt. 4,381 feet. Cheyenne County. Two hotels, 1 garage. Route marked through town and county, signs at town limits. One railroad, 1 express company, 1 telephone company,

DIX STATION

N.Y. **S.F.**

1888 **1443**

10

Pop. 26. Kimball County. 1 hotel, no garage. Gas and oil to be obtained at hotel. Local speed limit, 25 miles per hour. Route marked through town and county. Extensive road improvement completed in 1915. One railroad.

KIMBALL

N.Y. **S.F.**

1898 **1433**

11

Pop. 1,000. Alt. 4,697 feet. County seat, Kimball County. Two hotels, 2 garages. Route marked through town and county; signs at town limits. Two banks, 1 railroad, 25 general business places, 1 express company, 1 telephone company, 1 newspaper, 2 public schools, electric lights, water works. Commercial Club. Irrigation is extensively practiced. L. H. County Consul, B. K. Bushee.

BUSHNELL

N.Y. **S.F.**

1909 **1422**

11

Pop. 100. Kimball County. One hotel, 1 garage. Railroad station, 1 express company, 1 telephone company, 1 bank, 12 business places.

Wyoming

PAYSON W. SPAULDING, STATE CONSUL, EVANSTON, WYO.

GENERAL INFORMATION

THE name is taken from the Indian, meaning "big plains." The elevation of this state averages between 5,000 and 7,000 feet above the sea and it is traversed by the main chains of the Rocky Mountains, some of the peaks of which reach an altitude of 14,000 feet in this state.

The first white settlement was at old Fort Laramie on the North Platte River, and was established in 1834.

The Lincoln Highway through Wyoming was proclaimed a State Highway by former Governor Carey. Despite the vast area of the State, and the small population, a great deal has been done to improve the route. The tourist will note the principal activity in this direction has been the elimination of right angle turns, thus straightening the road. Generally speaking the native soil furnishes an excellent road bed, and much dragging and grading have been done to put it in good condition. The highest altitude reached is 8,347 feet at Sherman Hill where the Continental Divide is crossed. Eastern tourists driving through Wyoming on the Lincoln Highway will find objects of interest at every point through the state.

PINE BLUFFS

N.Y. **S.F.** Pop. 400. Alt. 5,042 feet. Laramie County.

1920 **1411** Two hotels, 1 garage. Local speed limit 15 miles per hour, enforced. Route marked through town and county. One bank, 1 railroad, 29 general business places, 1 express **10** company, 1 telephone company, 1 newspaper, 1 public school, electric lights, water works. Commercial Club.

EGBERT

N.Y. **S.F.** Pop. 75. Laramie County.

1930 **1401** One hotel, 1 garage. Route marked through town and county. One railroad, 1 express company, 1 telephone **6** company.

BURNS

N.Y. **S.F.** Pop. 150. Laramie County.

1936 **1395** Two hotels, 2 garages, 1 bank, 1 railroad, 18 general business places, 1 express company, 1 telephone company, 1 **17** newspaper, 1 public school, water works. Commercial Club.

ARCHER

N.Y. **S.F.** Pop. 15. Alt. 6,005 feet. Laramie County.

1953 **1378** No hotel, but meals and lodging can be obtained. Route marked through village and county. Extensive road improvement completed in 1915. One railroad, 1 express **9** company, 1 telephone company, 1 public school. Camp site.

Wyoming

CHEYENNE

N.Y. **S.F.**
1962 **1369**

6

Pop. 13,000. Alt. 6,054 feet. County seat, Laramie County. Capital of Wyoming.

Nine hotels, 5 garages. Local speed limit 10, 15 and 20 miles per hour, enforced. Route marked through city and county, signs at city limits. Extensive road improvement completed in 1915. Four banks, 3 railroads, 200 general business places, 4 express companies, 2 telephone companies, 2 newspapers, 7 public schools, electric lights, trolley, water works. Automobile Club, Commercial Club. Good camp site, good fishing, beautiful mountain scenery. A $400,000 federal building, Carnegie library, 4 public parks, beautiful lake drives on natural granite roads.
H. Local Consul, H. P. Hynds.

The first one of the five State Capitals to rename streets traversed by the Lincoln Highway, "Lincoln Highway" by official resolution.

Near Cheyenne is located Fort D. A. Russell, a military post, consisting of one regiment of infantry, two batteries of field artillery, one squadron of cavalry and a full hospital corps—about 2,200 men—with a large riding school, a target range, and a tract twenty miles square for field maneuvers, three miles from the city.

About the 27th of August of each year occurs the "Frontier Day," which celebration lasts for three days, during which thousands of cow-boys and many cow girls take part in prize contests in broncho busting,

Wyoming

roping steers, races and all sorts of western games and feats of skill. The stranger should not miss this if it is at all possible to arrange the tour to strike Cheyenne at the proper time. A few more years and the cow-boys will have become a thing of the past. The romance of the wild western life is fading away, until scarce a remnant is left for the traveler to see.

Note to Both East and West Bound Tourists.

West-bound:—Here detour for Denver, Colorado, via Wellington (34 mi.) Fort Collins (46 mi.) Loveland (59 mi.) and Longmont (78 mi.) to Denver (114 mi.). From Denver many points of interest and natural beauty may be reached. Among them are: Colorado Springs, Garden-of-the-Gods, Pikes Peak, Estes Park, Long's Peak, Cherokee Park, etc. If you plan to continue your route to Pacific Coast points, return over the same route (which is by far the best) to Cheyenne. Detour at Cheyenne for Cherokee (18 mi.). Follow the Blue Band marking.

East-bound:—Here detour for Denver and Colorado points (see preceding paragraph for detail.) If your plans contemplate proceeding east over the Lincoln Highway, two routes present themselves as follows:—Return from Denver to Cheyenne (114 mi.) or proceed direct from Denver to Big Springs, Nebraska, (227 mi.) via Fort Lupton, Greely, Fort Morgan, Sterling and Julesburg. Upon reaching either Cheyenne or Big Springs, proceed east following the route of the Lincoln Highway as shown in this Guide Book.

Between CHEYENNE and LARAMIE the tourist encounters much really excellent naturally graveled roads.

CORLETT STA.

N.Y. **S.F.** Laramie County.

1968 **1363** No tourist accommodations. Railroad station, telegraph. Drinking water, radiator water.

4

BORIE STA.

N.Y. **S.F.** Laramie County.

1972 **1359** No tourist accommodations. Railroad station, telegraph. Drinking water, radiator water.

4

OTTO STA.

N.Y. **S.F.** Laramie County.

1976 **1355** No tourist accommodations. Railroad station, telegraph. Drinking water, radiator water.

4

Wyoming

GRANITE CANYON STA.

N.Y. **S.F.** Pop. 29. Alt. 7,314 feet. Laramie County.
1980 **1351** No tourist accommodations. Railroad station, 1 express company, 1 telephone company. Drinking water, radiator
9 wateʀ. Good granite abounds here.

BUFORD

N.Y. **S.F.** Pop. 80. Alt. 7,780 feet. Albany County.
1989 **1342** No tourist accommodations.
Route marked through town and county. One general business place, 1 railroad, 1 express company, 1 telephone company, 1 public school. Beautiful scenery.
6 A telegraph station from which can be seen the "Twin Mountains" two peaks in the Black Hills, near which the noted desperado, Jack Slade, once had his retreat.

SHERMAN HILL (Hermosa R. R. Sta.)

N.Y. **S.F.** Pop. 40. Alt. 8,247 feet. Albany County.
1995 **1336** No tourist accommodations. Store and blacksmith shop. Gas oil and supplies may be obtained.
19 The Highway passes close to the famous Ames monument, 65 feet in height, erected to the memory of Oakes and Oliver Ames, to whose efforts the completion of the U. P. R. R. was mainly due. The view from this site is inspiring. To the south, Long's Peak in Colorado is visible.

Wyoming

OLD FORT SANDERS.

Old Fort Sanders is two and a half miles east of Laramie. The old fort was established in 1866 to protect the builders of the Union Pacific Railroad, and the men who were chopping ties on Elk Mountain, from the Indians. The old brick building was the guard house in which at one time 40 desperadoes were confined. The large frame house was the officers' quarters and here, at one time, were Grant, Sherman, Dodge and others. A monument near the road has been placed by the Daughters of the American Revolution to mark this historic spot.

LARAMIE

N.Y. S.F. Pop. 8,500. Alt. 7,153 feet. County seat, Albany County.

2014 1317 Five hotels, 3 garages. Local speed limit 12 miles per hour, enforced. Route marked through city and county, signs at city limits. Extensive road improvement completed in 1915. Three banks, 2 railroads, 300 general business places, 1 express company, 2 telephone companies, 2 newspapers, 4 public schools. Commercial Club. Good hunting and trout fishing, good camp site. L. H. Local Consuls, Elmer Lovejoy, John Campbell, Secretary Commercial Club.

19 Among the industries of Laramie are the railroad shops for the Laramie-Rawlins section of the Wyoming division, employing from 150 to 200 skilled mechanics; the rolling mills, which employ several hundred men; cement and brick plants; stock yards; an electric light plant, planing mill and 2 lumber yards; stone quarry; huge reservoirs where immense crops of ice are harvested. The University of Wyoming—including the State Agricultural College, the School of Mines, the United States Experiment Station, the Wyoming State Normal School, the Wyoming State School of Music and the University preparatory school—is located here. A federal building costing $100,000 and a library building costing $20,000 have recently been completed.

This is the educational center of Wyoming, having many State and other schools. It is the headquarters for hunting and fishing in the mountains of the west.

Note.—Here an alternate route to Rawlins is offered via Elk Mountain. This route offers many attractions to the tourist, sportsman and photographer. The distance to Rawlins being about 18 miles shorter than via Medicine Bow. Route well marked. There are about 32 gates to open on the Elk mountain route.

From LARAMIE to MEDICINE BOW the roads are generally level, some dirt and gravel, some have been graded, showing the possibility of improved roads by the skillful treatment of the native material.

Wyoming

BOSLER

N.Y. **S.F.** Pop. 75. Albany County.

2033 **1298** One garage. Route marked through town and county; signs at approach of town. Extensive road improvement completed in 1915. One railroad crossing at grade, not **5** protected. One railroad, 3 general business places, 1 express company, 1 telephone company, 1 newspaper, 2 public schools. Good hunting and fishing. Camp site.

COOPER LAKE

N.Y. **S.F.** Alt. 7,073 feet. Albany County.

2038 **1293** Nothing but a section house; no accommodations for tourists. Drinking water, radiator water and camp site. **3**

LOOKOUT

N.Y. **S.F.** Alt. 7,172 feet. Albany County.

2041 **1290** Railroad. No accommodations for tourists. Drinking and radiator water can be obtained. Camp site. There are sev- **6** eral large stock ranches near here.

HARPER

N.Y. **S.F.** Albany County.

2047 **1284** No tourist accommodations. Railroad section house. Drinking water, radiator water, camp site. **5**

ROCK RIVER

N.Y. **S.F.** Pop. 200. Alt. 6,904 feet. Albany County.

2052 **1279** One hotel, 1 garage. Local speed limit 15 miles per hour, enforced. Route marked through town and county. Extensive road improvement completed in 1915. One bank, **20** 1 railroad, 9 general business places, 1 express company, 1 telephone company, 1 public school, water works. Camp site, good fishing.

MEDICINE BOW

N.Y. **S.F.** Pop. 150. Alt. 6,566 feet. Carbon County.

2072 **1259** Two hotels, 1 garage. Route marked through town and county; signs at approach of town. One railroad cross-

Wyoming

5 ing at grade, not protected. One bank, 1 railroad, 1 express company, 1 telephone company, 1 public school. Camp site, good trout fishing. Local Consul, Gus Grimm.

The Virginian Hotel takes its name from Owen Wister's novel of that name, the manuscript having been written here.

Road marked at this point for Yellowstone Park. Good roads are reported. Ask L. H. Consul as to road conditions.

Fifty miles to the northeast lies Laramie Peak (11,000 ft.) and 20 miles to the southwest is Elk Mountain (11,162 ft.) which can be seen from the Highway all the way to Hanna and Fort Fred Steel.

ALLEN STA.

N.Y.   **S.F.**   Carbon County.

2077   **1254**   No tourist accommodations. Railroad station, telegraph. Drinking water, radiator water. Camp fire.

17

HANNA

N.Y.   **S.F.**   Pop. 2,000. Alt. 6,769 feet. Carbon County. One hotel.

2094   **1237**   Route marked through town and county. One railroad crossing at grade, not protected. One railroad, 7 general

22   business places, 1 express company, 1 telephone company, 1 public school, electric lights. Camp site. Extensive coal deposits in the neighborhood.

FT. STEELE

N.Y.   **S.F.**   Pop. 200. Alt. 6,510 feet. Carbon County.

2116   **1215**   One hotel. Route marked through town and county. One railroad crossing at grade, not protected. One railroad, 4 general business places, 1 express company, 1 telephone company, 1 public school. Camp site. Good trout fishing. Near this point are the Saratoga Hot Springs, a favorite resort for invalids, the waters being heavily charged with

7   medicinal properties. Fort Steele was established on June 30, 1868, by Colonel R. I. Dodge, of the Thirteenth U. S. Infantry, and it afforded a good strategic point, as well as a convenient base of supplies, in the wars with the Indians. This post was abandoned in 1886, only an agent being left to protect the Government property.

LAKOTA

N.Y.   **S.F.**   Carbon County.

2123   **1208**   No tourist accommodations. Railroad section house. Drinking water, radiator water.

4

GRANVILLE

N.Y.   **S.F.**   No tourist accommodations.

2127   **1204**   Railroad pumping house. Drinking water, radiator water.

6

Wyoming

RAWLINS

N.Y.	S.F.	
2133	1198	Pop. 4,200. Alt. 6,748 feet. County seat, Carbon County.
	30	Three hotels, 3 garages. Local speed limit 12 miles per hour, not enforced. Route marked through town and county. Three banks, 2 railroads, 30 general business places, 1 express company, 2 telephone companies, 2 newspapers, 3 public schools, electric lights, water works. Camp site. Local Consul, Dr. Barbour. County Consul, J. M. Rumsey.

Between this point and Yellowstone Park there is a road passing through Lander, thence to the southern boundary of Yellowstone Park. It is reported by those having first-hand information that this route to Yellowstone Park is less desirable than the one entering the Park from the West via Granger, Wyoming, Pocatello, Idaho, thence directly to the western entrance to Yellowstone Park, where there are accommodations for tourists, etc .

From RAWLINS TO POINT OF ROCKS;—excellent roads in fair weather.

CRESTON STA.

N.Y.	S.F.	
2163	1168	Alt. 7,043 feet. Sweetwater County.
	4	No tourist accommodations. Railroad station, telegraph. Drinking water, radiator water.

LATHAM STA.

N.Y.	S.F.	
2167	1164	Sweetwater County.
	8	No tourist accommodations. Railroad station, telegraph. Drinking water, radiator water.

WAMSUTTER

N.Y.	S.F.	
2175	1156	Pop. 125. Alt. 6,702 feet. Sweetwater County.
	35	One hotel, 1 garage. Route marked through town and county. Extensive road improvement completed in 1915. One railroad, 1 express company, 1 telephone company. Camp site.

Wyoming

This point was formerly called Washakie. Fort Washakie was a prominent military post on the Soshone and Arapahoe Indian Reservation.

POINT OF ROCKS

N.Y.   **S.F.**   Pop. 50. Alt. 6,512 feet. Sweetwater County.
2210   **1121**   One hotel, 1 railroad, 1 express company, 1 telephone company. Camp site.

          There are many mineral springs in this vicinity—iron, sulphur, magnesia and soda. Extensive coal mines are located near this point, from which many carloads are shipped daily. On the bluffs near Point of Rocks, just above a coal vein, Professor Hayden says, "is a seam of oyster shells six inches in thickness, which is an extinct **7** and undescribed species about the size of our common edible one." The sandstone bluffs at points along the road are worn by the action of the elements into curious fantastic shapes, some of which have been named, "Cave of the Sand," "Hermit's Grotto," "Water Washed Caves of the Fairies," "Sancho's Bower," etc.

THAYER JUNCTION

N.Y.   **S.F.**   Pop. 20. Railroad station. Sweetwater County.
2217   **1114**   No tourist accommodations. One small store, 1 express company, 1 telephone company. Drinking and radiator
  18   water.

Wyoming

ROCK SPRINGS

N.Y. S.F.
2235 1096

16

Pop. 7,500. Alt. 6,264 feet. Sweetwater County. Three hotels, 2 garages. Local speed limit, 8 miles per hour, enforced. Route marked through town and county; signs at town limits. Extensive road improvement. One railroad crossing at grade, protected. Three banks, 1 railroad, 7 general business places, 1 express company, 1 telephone company, 3 newspapers, 8 public schools, electric lights, water works. Automobile Club. Camp site. County Consul, John Hay. Local Consul, Dr. Lozier.

Large coal mining industry is found at Rock Springs. The mines employ about 3,000 men, and produce many million tons of coal annually. Rock Springs was named after a saline spring of water which boils up near the foot of the bluff. An artesian well was sunk at this point, 1,145 feet deep. The Wyoming Hospital and other state buildings are located here. From this point to Green River the scenery is grand and impressive.

Between this point and Yellowstone Park there is a road passing through Lander, thence to the southern boundary of Yellowstone Park. It is reported by those having first-hand information that this route to Yellowstone Park is less desirable than the one entering the Park from the West via Granger, Wyoming, Pocatello, Idaho, thence directly to the western entrance to Yellowstone Park, where there are accommodations for tourists, etc.

Note—Pinedale, 100 miles north, is said to rival Yellowstone Park in natural scenery. Streams are bridged. Fremont Lake, 17 miles long, affords excellent fishing and camping. Good roads.

ROCK SPRING TO GREEN RIVER. Road well graded and graveled.

GREEN RIVER

N.Y. S.F.
2251 1080

15

Pop. 1,800. Alt. 6,083 feet. County seat, Sweetwater County.

Four hotels, 2 garages, auto supplies, tires, repair shop. Local speed limit 15 miles per hour, enforced. Route marked through town and county; signs at town limits.

Wyoming

One railroad crossing at grade, protected. Two banks, 2 railroads, 15 general business places, 1 express company, 2 telephone companies, 1 newspaper, 1 public school, electric lights, water works. Commercial Club. Numerous good camp sites. Good hunting and fishing. Interesting scenery. L. H. Local Consul, Hugo Gaenseller.

This point is situated on Green River, which about 150 miles south unites with the Grand and becomes the Colorado River. About three miles west of Green River is the famous Fish Cut. Here, in 1890, a geological expedition headed by Prof. O. C. Marsh, of Yale College, found petrified fish in abundance, and a small bed containing fossil insects.

From Green River, good road to Pinedale and Fremont Lake for excellent trout fishing and big game hunting and camping.

From GREEN RIVER to LYMAN the roads vary from fairly well graveled to clay.

BRYAN STA.

N.Y. S.F. Alt. 6,191 feet. Sweetwater County.
2266 1065 No tourist accommodations. Railroad station, telegraph.
19 Drinking water, radiator water.

GRANGER

N.Y. S.F. Granger is three-fourths of a mile off the Lincoln Highway to the north.
2285 1046 Pop. 100. Alt. 6,284 feet. Sweetwater County.
30 Two hotels, 2 railroads, 2 general business places, 1 express company, 1 telegraph company, 1 public school. Camp site.

The road leading north and west, open to tourists, via Pocatello is reported to be the most desirable route for motorists contemplating a visit to Yellowstone National Park. First-hand information as to this route indicates that the road via Pocatello leads directly to an official entrance at which will be found all tourist conveniences. It is also said that from this point the road to Glacier, Montana, is the best.

It is suggested that tourists contemplating a trip to Glacier National Park communicate with the President of the Commercial Club of Darby, Montana, who will furnish maps and other information of value.

LYMAN

N.Y. S.F. Pop. 800. Uinta County.
2315 1016 Two hotels. Route marked through town and county.
6 Three general business places, telephone, 1 newspaper, 2 public schools. Camp site. Mormon settlement.

From LYMAN to EVANSTON the roads vary from good gravel to good dirt, well graded.

125

Wyoming

FT. BRIDGER

N.Y. **S.F.** Pop. 100. Alt. 7,000 feet. Uinta County.

2321 **1010** One hotel, 1 garage. Route marked through town and county; signs at town limits. Telephone, 1 public school, 1 general business place. The road turns square here. On the left is a large house at which meals may be obtained. By walking straight ahead through the lane and trees you will pass on the right, old officers' quarters, and immediately beyond enter the old parade grounds.

Ft. Bridger is located on the Black Fork of the Green River, where the stream branches into three channels, forming several large islands.

35 Jim Bridger built this fort in 1834 and for a long time it remained one of the most important of the many trading posts in the far west. It was built of logs with sod roof and was surrounded by a heavy fence of pointed timbers eight feet high for protection against the Indians.

In 1853 it was abandoned; the owners being driven out by the Mormons.

Many wild and bloody scenes were enacted here between the trappers and the Indians.

It was here that General Johnson rebuilt the fort and quartered his army in 1857 when operating against the Mormons. The officers' quarters, the old guard house and some of the other buildings are still standing as left by General Johnson, and in June the parade ground is covered with beautiful, wild Iris flowers.

EVANSTON

N.Y. **S.F.** Pop. 3,000. Alt. 6,300 feet. County seat, Uinta County.

2356 **975** Three hotels, 2 garages. Route marked through town and county; signs at town limits. One railroad crossing at grade, protected. Three banks, 1 railroad, 1 express company, 2 telephone companies, 2 newspapers, 4 public schools, electric lights, water works. Commercial Club. L. H State Consul, Payson W. Spaulding.

3 Evanston is situated in Bear River Valley. It has a new $12,000 high school; flour mill; ice storage plant, 18,000 tons capacity; a city park, machine shops, a new $200,000 federal building. The city is the seat of the State Insane Asylum and the United States Land Office. It is also headquarters for oil men. Coal fields cover a large extent of territory.

Wyoming

NATIONAL PARK REGULATIONS

Under stringent restrictions motorists are permitted access to Yellowstone Park. The regulations governing the admission of motor cars to this Park are so involved and lengthy that their complete reproduction is not permitted, due to limited space. The Department of the Interior, at Washington, D. C., will furnish copies of the regulations, or they may be obtained while in San Francisco. Briefly outlined the regulations are as follows:—

1. Motor cycles are not permitted.

2. A fee of $5.00 for a single round trip, payable in cash at the station in Yosemite Valley is exacted. $1.00 additional fee is collected from motor cars entering the Mariposa Grove of Big Trees.

3. There are numerous restrictions as to gears, brakes, muffler cutouts, rates of speed, the meeting of teams, checking of automobiles, fines and penalties.

4. The Department has prepared a series of schedules and general instructions as to touring, hours of arrival and departure, etc.

The publishers of this guide suggest personal application by letter to the Department of the Interior, Washington, D. C., for rules governing not only Yosemite Park, but Yellowstone Park, Glacier Park, the Grand Canyon, and other National Parks and Forest Reserves.

Shipment of Cars

WHEN you arrive on the coast and contemplate your return to your home city the following alternatives present themselves for your consideration:

1. Return over the Lincoln Highway.
2. Return over one of the other routes, or
3. Return home by train, shipping your car by freight.

The latter course will be followed by many and it is to these tourists that we commend the following procedure:

It will be very expensive to ship your car by itself. If grouped in a carload shipment you can save from 25% to 50% of the individual rate. For example: The rates for single automobile shipment from Oakland (R. R. terminal) to Chicago is $6.80 per hundred (minimum weight 2000 lbs.) The cost of this light weight car would be $136. If in a carload shipment the rate is $3.00 per hundred or $60 for a car of 2000 lbs. (minimum weight); a saving of $76. To group cars as to destination involves some expense in handling, storage, etc. It is safe to assume a saving of from 25% to 50% on each car shipped, when grouped or pooled with other cars for the same destination.

The Association has been asked for information regarding this important matter, and is pleased to announce an arrangement whereby your troubles are minimized and the expense greatly reduced.

When you know approximately the date of your arrival on the coast and when you would want your car shipped, write to our representative in care of the Lawrence Warehouse Co., at Oakland, California, be specific as to the information that will enable him to complete arrangements that will agree with your plans.

Points of destination should be major cities nearest your home as: Boston, New York, Albany, Philadelphia, Richmond, Detroit, etc.

It is suggested that shipment be made to these or other common points, and that you arrange to meet your car on its arrival there, and drive to your home town or city.

As these are consolidated shipments, arrange to ship to the nearest common terminal point, thus insuring prompt service.

The Lawrence Warehouse Co. insure all cars while in their possession; load them; see that they are made secure in the freight cars; secure receipts from the R. R. companies, in fact they relieve you of all of the many troublesome details of dealing with the transportation companies. They have the organization and equipment and can give you the service. Cars for shipment east, middle west, or other points to be delivered to the Company at the Pacsteel Station, Oakland.

Utah

LINCOLN HIGHWAY STATE CONSUL, CHARLES TYNG,
Salt Lake City

GENERAL INFORMATION:

THE Lincoln Highway tourist will find much of interest in crossing this state. West of Salt Lake City a view of the great Salt Lake will be obtained, and the tourist is in sight of the mountains and does some traveling over mountain roads in the western part of the state. The roadway is mainly native of soil, and will be found to range from fair to excellent. The Lincoln Highway is the main travel road across the state, and when the weather is particularly dry it is liable to be cut up and rough in spots. Extended improvements are contemplated during the coming year and the tourist should encounter no difficulties on the route. In the past, motorists have shown some hesitancy about making the trip from Salt Lake City to Ely, Nevada, crossing a small part of the desert, because of the promiscuous circulation of advice as to extra equipment which should be carried. It is advisable to take a thermos bottle of iced water, or a desert water bag and some food in case one is held up with tire or engine trouble, but other than that no extras are needed.

WYUTA STA.
N.Y. **S.F.** Rich County.
2359 **972** Railroad station, drinking water, radiator water, telegraph.

5

WASATCH
N.Y. **S.F.** Pop. 10. Alt. 6,828 feet. Summit County.
2364 **967** Route marked through county. Railroad station, express
8 company, telephone company, 1 railroad crossing at grade, not protected.

CASTLE ROCK
N.Y. **S.F.** Pop. 20. Alt. 6,240 feet. Summit County.
2372 **959** Railroad station, meals, ranch lodgings, gas, oil, express
7 company, telephone, telegraph, post office. Route marked through county, signs at approach to village. Beautiful mountain scenery.

EMORY STATION
N.Y. **S.F.** Summit County.
2379 **952** U. P. Section house. No accommodations for tourists.
9 Drinking water, radiator water, telegraph.

MAIN FORKS
N.Y. **S.F.** Summit County.
2388 **943** No town. No accommodations for tourists. Pass under
5 railroad, take first road to left. (Echo, one-quarter mile to right.)

Utah

COALVILLE

N.Y. **S.F.** Pop. 976. Alt. 5,591 feet. County seat, Summit County.
2393 **938** Two hotels, 2 garages. Local speed limit 10 miles per hour. Route marked through town and county, signs at town limits. One railroad, 1 express company, 1 telegraph com-
3 pany, telephone, beautiful scenery. Good fishing. Good graded road to Wanship, but not surfaced, and muddy in wet weather.

HOYTSVILLE

N.Y. **S.F.** Pop. 108. Summit County. On the Weber River.
2396 **935** Good fishing and camp site. Railroad station.

5

WANSHIP

N.Y. **S.F.** Pop. 118. Alt 5,859 feet. Summit County.
2401 **930** One hotel, 1 garage. Route marked through town and county, signs at town limits. One railroad, 1 express company, 1 telegraph company, telephone. Good graded road up Silver Creek, winding and dangerous in wet weather. From Wanship to Salt Lake after leaving the canyon the
10 road is gravel formation to the Summit. Ranch houses with phones at frequent intervals and would afford night stops. Summit to Salt Lake down Parleys canyon, graded road, hard surfaced and good going even when wet.

KIMBALL'S RANCH

N.Y. **S.F.** Summit County.
2411 **920** Meals, lodging, telephone.

10

ROACH'S RANCH

N.Y. **S.F.** Summit County.
2421 **910** Meals, lodging, telephone.

17

SALT LAKE CITY

N.Y. **S.F.** Pop. 102,000. Alt. 4,268 feet. County seat Salt Lake
2438 **893** County. Capital of Utah.
Six large hotels, many smaller ones, ten garages. Local speed limit, 8 and 15 miles per hour, enforced. Route marked through county. One railroad crossing at grade, protected. Fourteen banks, 5 railroads, 3 express companies, 2 telephone companies, 4 newspapers, 36 public schools. Automobile Club, Commercial Club, L. H. State Consul, Charles Tyng.
15 The home of the Mormon Church (Latter Day Saints). The Temple, the Tabernacle and other Mormon institutional buildings are wonderful as examples of Ecclesiastical Architecture. The organ in the Mormon Tabernacle is one of the world's wonders. Liberty Park is also one of the attractions, as it contains the original buildings erected by Brigham Young.

Utah

The Tabernacle, built in 1864-67, is an extraordinary
structure and the interior exhibits one of the largest
unsupported arches in the world.

The Temple lies just to the east of this building and
was constructed in 1853-93, costing over $4,000,000.

Many short tours may be made in various directions
from the city, and much wonderful scenery is within
easy reach of the motorist.

The capital of the Mormon settlement, was founded
upon the arrival of that sect in the valley of the Great
Salt Lake, in 1847. It is almost surrounded by lofty
mountains, in which are carved many magnificent
canyons. It is situated at the foot of the western
slope of the Wasatch Mountains, whose heights form
the western boundary of the great basin and embrace
the valley on the north and east.

To the west and northwest opens out the great
desert, with the Great Salt Lake in the center and
but twelve miles away.

The growth of this delightful mountain city, in its
arid, desolate situation, is a monument to the untiring
energy and devotion to principle which has no parallel
in history.

Ages ago the Great Salt Lake was a fresh water
inland sea of 1,200 feet in depth, with an outlet to the
Pacific Ocean through the Snake River. Through
evaporation the lake has grown smaller and smaller,
until now there is no outlet and the salt in the water
has increased to 25 per cent. The ocean contains but
three to four per cent, and the Dead Sea 24 per cent
in comparison. The water is extremely bouyant and
a novel bath may be had at this Salt-Air bathing resort.

SALT LAKE CITY to TIMPIE.

Conditions of this section of the road is governed more
or less by the weather conditions. It is generally good and is
of gravel, sand and adobe.

PLEASANT GREEN (EAST GARFIELD)
2453   **878**   Salt Lake County.

    2   Route marked through county. Drinking water, radiator
water, telephone, telegraph, post office, camp site.

Utah

RAGTOWN (Italian Miner Settlement)

N.Y. **S.F.** Salt Lake County.

2455 **876** No accommodations for tourists.

3

GARFIELD

N.Y. **S.F.** Pop. 600. Salt Lake County.

2458 **873** Company House of Utah Copper Mines will furnish meals and lodging. Route marked through county. Three railroads, 1 express company, 1 telegraph company, telephone, **8** post office, camp site. Ore mills viewed on special permit only.

LAKEPOINT

N.Y. **S.F.** Pop. 230. Tooele County.

2466 **865** Ranch meals and lodgings. Route marked through village and county, signs at approach of village. One railroad, 1 general business place, 2 public schools. Lakepoint **2** is on the shore of Great Salt Lake and a splendid view of the lake is had.

MILLTOWN

N.Y. **S.F.** Tooele County.

2468 **863** Ranch meals and lodging, drinking water, radiator water.

10

GRANTSVILLE

N.Y. **S.F.** Pop. 1,154. Tooele County.

2478 **853** Three hotels. No local speed limit, but excessive speed prohibited. Route marked through town and county, signs at town limits. One bank, 1 railroad, 7 general business **14** places, 2 express companies, 1 telegraph company, telephone, 1 newspaper, 3 public schools, electric lights, water works. Commercial Club. Grantsville Forest Reserve 4 miles southwest of city.

Utah

TIMPIE POINT (Only a landmark)
N.Y. **S.F.** Tooele County.
2492 **839** Railroad station one mile to west in sight. No accommodations for tourists.

16

IOSEPA
N.Y. **S.F.** Pop. 125. Tooele County.
2508 **823** Accommodations furnished tourists by Manager of the Iosepa Agricultural & Stock Co. Ranch meals and lodgings. Route marked through village and county. General store, telephone, 1 public school. Hawaiian settlement. Native dances are sometimes held.

7

BROWN'S RANCH
N.Y. **S.F.** Tooele County.
2515 **816** Ranch meals and lodgings, drinking water, radiator water, supplies.

2

INDIAN RANCH
N.Y. **S.F.** Tooele County.
2517 **814** Garage and eating house. Good food. Comfortable sleeping quarters. Limited supply of accessories. Camp site.

5

INDIAN FARM OR SEVERE FARM
N.Y. **S.F.** Tooele County.
2522 **809** Ranch meals and lodging. Drinking water, radiator water.

3

ORR'S RANCH
N.Y. **S.F.** Excellent ranch meals and lodging. Drinking water, radiator water. L. H. Local Consul, Hamilton Orr.
2525 **806**

17

ORR'S RANCH to FISH SPRINGS

Some difficulties may be encountered on this part of the road. If traveling in wet weather advice should be sought at Orr's before making this start.

COUNTY WELL
N.Y. **S.F.** Just a well. Radiator water only.
2542 **789**

42

Utah

FISH SPRINGS (J. J. THOMAS RANCH)

N.Y.   **S.F.**   Alt. 6,269 feet. Juab County.

2584   **747**   Ranch meals and lodging. Hot sulphur springs close to ranch.

    20   If trouble is experienced, build a sage brush fire. Mr. Thomas will come with a team. He can see you 20 miles off.

FISH SPRINGS to KEARNEY'S RANCH

There is a seven-mile section between these points that is liable to be bad in wet weather, otherwise the road will be found to be acceptable.

CALLAO (KEARNEY'S RANCH)

N.Y.   **S.F.**   Pop. 25. Juab County.

2604   **727**   Ranch meals and lodging.

    26

KEARNEY'S RANCH to IBAPAH.

Care should be exercised as washes are liable to be encountered, which if taken at too great speed, are liable to break a spring.

IBAPAH (SHERIDAN'S RANCH)

N.Y.   **S.F.**   Pop. 35. Tooele County.

2630   **701**   One hotel, excellent ranch meals and lodging. One garage. One general business place, 1 public school.

    25

IBAPAH to ELY.

Ninety per cent excellent natural gravel, the remainder fair.

Nevada

LINCOLN HIGHWAY STATE CONSUL, G. S. HOAG,
Ely, Nevada

GENERAL INFORMATION

NEVADA was originally a part of California. The name is taken from the Spanish meaning "snowy;" but it is commonly known as the "Sage Brush State." It is one of the most important states in the Union from the point of mineral wealth.

There are numerous parallel ranges of mountains running north and south through the state, each one of which the tourist has to cross. Some of these ranges rise more than 9,000 feet above the sea.

The great Comstock Lode at Virginia City near Reno was discovered in 1859 and miners flocked into the district from all over the country. The silver product of the state from 1859 to 1869 was $137,000,000 and this had much to do with gaining Nevada a place in the Union as a state in 1864.

The principal river is the Humboldt, called at one time the "Ogden River," and the old emigrant trails followed down this river from Fort Hall, Idaho, down to Carson Sink in the vicinity of Fallon, and these old trails struck the Lincoln Highway about the location of Fernley, 37 miles east of Reno.

In 1825 Peter Ogden visited the Humbolt River and in 1826 Jedediah Smith crossed the state from west to east. Fremont passed through the state in 1843-45, and in 1849 the Mormons founded a trading post on the Carson River near Wadsworth.

This state is the fourth in area in the Union, and has a population of less than 100,000. It has a wide range in elevation, which averages 4,000 feet. The unique feature of Nevada is the number of rivers and lakes which have no visible outlet. Nevada, except California, is said to have the greatest range of climate of any of the states in the Union. Its northern boundary corresponds with that of Pennsylvania, and its southern boundary with the northern line of Alabama. But a small percentage of the great area of the fertile soil of Nevada is under cultivation.

Tourists who have enjoyed the delights of European travel say that the natural scenery of the State of Nevada as it is viewed from the Lincoln Highway, is superior to that of practically any foreign country. The greatest elevation on the Lincoln Highway is said to be that of Austin Summit where the Highway for a short distance travels the Toyaibe Forest Reserve over a highway constructed by the Federal Government.

Nevada

TIPPETT

N.Y. S.F. Pop. 10. White Pine County.

2655　676 Meals, lodging. Camp site. Route marked through county. Extensive road improvement. General store.

22 Snowcapped Mt. Wheeler in sight to the south, 13,058 feet high.

ANDERSON'S RANCH

N.Y. S.F. White Pine County.

2677　654 Meals, lodging, gas, oil, drinking water, radiator water, camp site.
7

SCHELLBOURNE

N.Y. S.F. White Pine County.

2684　647 Ranch and postoffice, once a government post on the emigrant trail and pony express. Route marked across county.
20 Meals, lodging, drinking water, radiator water, camp site.

MAGNUSON'S RANCH

N.Y. S.F. White Pine County.

2704　627 Meals, lodging, gas, oil, drinking water, radiator water, camp site.
8

MCGILL

N.Y. S.F. Pop. 2,500. White Pine County.

2712　619 No hotels, several lodging and boarding houses. Route marked through town and county. One bank, 1 railroad, 25 general business places, 1 express company, 1 telegraph
11 company, telephone, 1 public school, electric lights, water works. Smelting plant which normally handles from 12,000 to 15,000 tons of copper ore per day.

EAST ELY

N.Y. S.F. Pop. 475. White Pine County.

2723　608 Two hotels, 1 garage. Route marked through town and county, signs at town limits. Extensive road improvement.
2 One railroad 1 express company, 1 telegraph company. Copper mining district.

Nevada

ELY

N.Y.	S.F.	
2725	606	Pop. 3,500. Alt. 6,000 feet. White Pine County. Six hotels, 1 garage. Local speed limit 12 miles per hour, not enforced. Route marked through town and county, signs at town limits. Extensive road improvement. Three banks, 1 railroad, 100 general business places, 1 express company, 1 telegraph company, 3 newspapers, 3 public schools, electric lights, water works. Automobile Club. Copper mining. Camp site. Picnic grounds. L. H. State Consul, G. S. Hoag. County Consul, Geo. Vanderhoff.
	3	

ELY to EUREKA.

Well sign-boarded.

LANE

N.Y.	S.F.	
2728	603	Pop. 100. White Pine County. Drinking water, radiator water, camp site, telephone, telegraph, 1 railroad. Mining town.
	5	

COPPER FLAT

N.Y.	S.F.	
2733	598	White Pine County. One railroad, meals, lodging, gas, oil, drinking water, radiator water, camp site, telephone, telegraph. Seat of big copper pit from which the ore is mined with steam shovels. Tourists should visit this copper mine.
	2	

REIPETOWN

N.Y.	S.F.	
2735	596	White Pine County. Railroad station, gas, drinking water, radiator water, telephone.
	1	

Nevada

KIMBERLY

N.Y.   **S.F.**   Pop. 300. White Pine County.

2736   **595**   Meals, lodging. Drinking water, radiator water, camp site, telephone. Copper mines. An interesting point to tarry.

     8

JAKE'S SUMMIT

N.Y.   **S.F.**   White Pine County.

2744   **587**   No accommodations.

     15

MOOREMAN'S RANCH

N.Y.   **S.F.**   White Pine County.

2759   **572**   Meals, lodging, gas, oil, drinking water, radiator water, camp site, telephone.

     2

ROSEVEAR'S RANCH

N.Y.   **S.F.**   White Pine County.

2761   **570**   Ranch not open. No accommodations.

     6

WHITE PINE SUMMIT

N.Y.   **S.F.**   White Pine County.

2767   **564**   No accommodations. Beautiful view from the point.

     10

SIX MILE HOUSE (COYLE'S RANCH)

N.Y.   **S.F.**   White Pine County.

2777   **554**   Meals, lodging, telephone, camp site.

     11

PANCAKE SUMMIT

N.Y.   **S.F.**   White Pine County.

2788   **543**   No accommodations.

     7

FOURTEEN MILE HOUSE

N.Y.   **S.F.**   White Pine County.

2795   **536**   Deserted. Water for radiator—do not drink.

     8

PINTO HOUSE

N.Y.   **S.F.**   Eureka County.

2803   **528**   Drinking water, radiator water, camp site.

     7

Nevada

EUREKA

N.Y.	S.F.	
2810	521	Pop. 785. Alt. 6,826 feet. County seat, Eureka County. Two hotels, 1 garage. Route marked through town and county, signs at town limits. Extensive road improvement. One railroad, 30 general business places, 1 express company, 1 telegraph company, 1 newspaper, 1 public school.
	69	Camp site. L. H. Local Consul, Rudolph Zadow. Eureka is one of the oldest mining camps in Nevada, being established in the early '70's, and has a record of producing $50,000,000 from the gold and silver mines.

EUREKA to AUSTIN.

Some hard road, some gravel, a number of washes, some rough spots and some mountain grades.

Water will be found six times. Well sign boarded. The drive takes about five hours.

AUSTIN

N.Y.	S.F.	
2879	452	Pop. 700. Alt. 6,594 feet. County seat, Lander County. Three hotels, 3 garages. Route marked through town and county, signs at town limits. One bank, 1 railroad, 20 business places, 1 express company, 1 telegraph company, 1 newspaper, 1 public school, water works, camp site. The
	26	town of Austin is situated in Pony canyon, in the Toiyabe mountain range, taking its name after the pony express

139

Nevada

riders, who carried the United States mail in relays from Omaha to Sacramento, Calif. L. H. Local Consul, William Easton. Austin is the distributing point for Central Nevada, and has an early mining camp history. It has produced many millions of dollars in silver and lead, and it is at present one of the best camps in Nevada. One of the historical points to be seen is the "Stokes' Castle," built by an eccentric and rich miner in the camp's boom days.

AUSTIN to FALLON.

Many miles of hard road, some good and some fair gravel; a number of washes and two alkali flats. Due to heavy teaming (ore) some of these will be found more or less cut up.

Use caution at Salt Wells, east of Fallon, if you approach in bad weather.

NEW PASS CANYON

N.Y.   S.F. Churchill County.

2905   426 Drinking water, radiator water, camp site.

20

ALPINE RANCH

N.Y.   S.F. Churchill County.

2925   406 Meals, lodging, gas, oil, drinking water, radiator water, camp site. Williams ranch belonging to Williams' estate, Nevada. Mr. Willaims' son says that 20 miles from here **13** is a miniature of the Grand Canyon of Colorado, which is almost identical to the larger canyon of Arizona and equally as beautiful. He suggests that tourists make inquiry any time it permits and that this detour be made.

EASTGATE (WILLIAMS RANCH)

N.Y.   S.F. Alt. 5,291 feet. Churchill County.

2938   393 Meals, lodging, gas, oil, drinking water, radiator water, camp site. A fine place to stop.

11

WESTGATE

N.Y.   S.F. Alt. 4,504 feet. Churchill County.

2949   382 Meals, gas, oil, drinking water, radiator water, camp site, telephone.

12

FRENCHMAN'S STA. (BERMOND'S)

N.Y.   S.F. Churchill County.

2961   370 Hotel, meals, lodging, gas, oil, camp site, telephone.

8

SAND SPRINGS

N.Y.   S.F. Alt. 3,926 feet. Churchill County.

2969   362 Lodging, meals, drinking water, radiator water, blacksmith shop, gas, telephone. West bound tourists should stop and **12** inquire best road to take.

Nevada

SALT WELLS

N.Y. **S.F.** Saloon. Ranch. Make inquiries here if in doubt. Drink-
2981 **350** ing water, radiator water, telephone, meals.

6

GRIMES RANCH

N.Y. **S.F.** Churchill County.
2987 **344** Meals, lodging, drinking water, radiator water, telephone,
gas.
8

FALLON

N.Y. **S.F.** Pop. 1,200. County seat, Churchill County.
2995 **336** Two hotels, 3 garages. Local speed limit 15 miles per
hour, enforced. Route marked through town, signs at
town limits. Some road improvement. One bank, 1 rail-
17 road, 1 express company, 1 telegraph company, 2 newspapers, 3 public schools, electric lights, water works. Commercial Club. Telephone. L. H. Local Consul, I. H. Kent.

Nevada

FALLON to WADSWORTH.

Some chuck holes. Some fine gravel.

At this point detour for the Government Reclamation Project, officially known as the Truckee-Carson Irrigation Project. There are two dams; the first one from Reno is known as the Derby Dam and is on the Truckee River, while the second and larger one, the Lahontan Dam, lies a few miles off the direct route to the south, between Fallon and Wadsworth. An inspection of these two dams is warranted. There are no tourist accommodations at either of the dams, Hazen, Fallon, Reno and Wadsworth, all near, have adequate accommodations for all tourists.

The Truckee-Carson project embraces about 206,000 acres. The farms are in units of approximately 80 acres each. The elevation is about 4,000 feet above sea level. Very little snow, which vanishes quickly. The water is derived from the combined flow of the Truckee and Carson rivers, being snow fed from the eastern slopes of the Sierra Nevada Mountains in California. The soil is extremely fertile and the crops are varied.

HAZEN

N.Y. S.F. Pop. 100. Churchill County.

3012   319   One hotel, 1 garage. Route marked through town, signs at town limits. One railroad, 8 general business places, 1 express company, 1 telegraph company, 1 public school, electric lights, water works. Camp site.

11   At this point the Western Ore Purchasing Company operates a sampling plant. Smelting grades of ore from all the big camps of Nevada are brought here for assay. Visitors should stop and watch this interesting operation of the mining industry.

FERNLEY

N.Y. S.F. Pop. 100. Lyon County.

3023   308   Located in the western part of the Truckee-Carson Irrigation Project. Meals, lodging. Some road improvement.

3   One railroad, 4 general business places, 1 express company, 1 telegraph company, long distance telephone, 1 public school, camp site.

WADSWORTH

N.Y. S.F. Pop. 1,309. Alt. 4,079 feet. Washoe County.

3026   305   Three hotels, 4 garages. Local speed limit 12 miles per hour, enforced. Route marked through town, signs at town limits. Extensive road improvement. One railroad

6   crossing at grade, protected by signals. One railroad, 3 general business places, 1 express company, 1 telegraph company, telephone, 2 public schools. Camp site.

Nevada

WADSWORTH to RENO.

Some good roads; frequent crossings of railroads.

DERBY

N.Y.	S.F.	
3032	299	Pop. 50. Washoe County. One hotel, 1 garage. Route marked through town, signs at town limits. One railroad, 1 general business place, telegraph, 1 public school.
	14	

VISTA

N.Y.	S.F.	
3046	285	Washoe County. Railroad station, drinking water, radiator water, telegraph.
	10	

SPARKS

N.Y.	S.F.	
3056	275	Pop. 2,500. Washoe County. Four hotels, 1 garage. Local speed limit 12 miles per hour, enforced. Route marked through town and county, signs at town limits. Extensive road improvement. One bank, 1 railroad, large railroad shops, 1 express company, 1 telegraph company, 1 newspaper, 1 public school, electric lights, trolley, water works.
	5	

Nevada

RENO

N.Y. **S.F.**
3061 **270**

Pop. 14,000. Alt. 4,499 feet. County seat, Washoe County. On the Truckee River.

Seventeen hotels, 5 garages. Local speed limit 12 miles per hour, enforced. Route marked through town, signs at town limits. Five banks, 3 railroads, 1 express company, 2 telegraph companies, telephone, 2 newspapers, 8 public schools, electric lights, trolley, water works. Automobile Club. Commercial Club. Camp site. L. H. Local Consuls, F. J. Byington, Mayor G. T. Stevenson.

12

Reno is a fine city, and one of the most prominent in the far west. Steamboat Springs, and the great Comstock Lode are within easy reach of Reno. The Comstock Lode has produced over one billion dollars in precious metals. It is here we turn south if following that arm of the Lincoln Highway which goes via Lake Tahoe. Both routes come together again at Sacramento, Calif.

To the west rises the great barrier of the Sierra Nevada (Snowy Range) Mountains, and in a few miles we are carried among the fir forests and to the high pass (Donner Pass) over the summit.

Eight miles from Reno is Steamboat Springs; one of the wonders of nature and one of the much spoken of points on the old trail in the days of the early explorers.

VERDI

N.Y. **S.F.**
3073 **258**

Pop. 156. Washoe County.

One railroad, 2 telegraph companies, 1 express company.

23

SENDING YOUR A[
At a Saving of 50% to 25% of

WHEN you return home, you no doubt pla[
by regular freight, you will not only have
your car for shipment, but you will be oblige[

By taking advantage of the service arrang[
pany—the official shippers of the Lincoln Hig[
all this trouble and bother, but you will save [

Warehouses

For your convenience, we provide warehouse facilities at principal Pacific
Coast cities at reasonable rates, if you should want to store your car.

Shipping Receipt

When your automobile is delivered to us, we issue you a receipt which
covers your car, all accessories and attachments; shows the weight and charges,
together with the name and address of the agent at the point of destination.

Lawrence System of Loading

The utmost
care is taken in
the loading of auto-
mobiles to insure
their safe arrival,
without injury, at
the destination.

LAWRE[

40[

JTOMOBILE HOME
the Regular Freight Charges

ı to travel by rail. If you ship your automobile
the bother and worry of preparing and loading
ı to pay the regular less-than-car-load rate.

:d for you by the Lawrence Warehouse Com-
ıway Association—you will not only be saved
rom 50% to 25% in transportation charges.

Sufficient space is left between machines to safeguard against chafing or
marring of parts.

The wheels or each automobile are carefully cradled with several thick-
nesses of burlap, providing perfect security, with sufficient elasticity to prevent
chafing. Blocks of special design are used, sawed to conform to the shape
of the wheel.

The wheels are anchored as shown in the illustration, so that the automobile is held securely in place while in transit.

Covers will be furnished, if desired.

Make Your Arrangements NOW

In order that we may give you the very best of service, we would request
that you communicate with us immediately. *Tell us the make and model of
your car; the point where you will turn it over to us; the destination of the
shipment and the probable date.*

We will then advise you the exact cost and give you any special information that you might desire.

Lawrence Service will save you time, money and bother. Plan to use it.

Address Lincoln Highway Representative, care of

ICE WAREHOUSE COMPANY
Executive Offices:

Eleventh Street, Oakland, California
Telephones: Lakeside 456 and 457

WINDOW THROUGH INSTRUMENT SHOWS THE FLUID AT NIGHT

DANGER, STOP YOUR CAR CYLINDERS AND BEARINGS OVERHEATING

YOU ARE OBTAINING THE BEST GASOLINE EFFICIENCY

GO AHEAD PLENTY OF WATER AND OIL

YOUR MOTOR IS COLD AND INEFFICIENT

DANGER! COVER YOUR RADIATOR TO PREVENT FREEZING

View From Seat

BOYCE
MOTO-METER
THE MOTOR HEAT INDICATOR

EVERY experienced transcontinental tourist appreciates the necessity of knowing the exact temperature condition of his motor. A **Boyce Moto-Meter** attached to the regular radiator cap of your car gives you this information while you drive.

Under general conditions its ever visible red indicator, showing a normal temperature, eliminates completely every source of worry, but the moment that abnormal conditions occur, the red column jumps to the "Danger" mark, warning the driver to stop. The first time you are warned that your radiator needs water or that your motor requires oil, the price of the instrument will be saved many times over.

When over twenty-seven of America's foremost automobile manufacturers adopt any new invention as a necessary part of their regular equipment, it is safe to assume that the device has merit and will do with reasonable certainty what its manufacturers claim for it. The **Boyce Moto-Meter** is regular equipment on the following cars:

Abbott-Detroit	Netco Trucks
Ahrens-Fox	Owen-Magnetic
Anderson	Packard
Biddle	Packard Trucks
Chalmers (Cabriolet)	Peerless
Crane-Simplex	Premier
F. R. P.	Peugeot
Haynes	Pennsey
Jeffery "6"	Simplex
Jeffery (Trucks)	Stutz
Lippard-Stewart	South Bend
Lexington	Sayers-Scovill
Mercer	Westcott
McFarlan	Glenn Martin Aeroplanes
Martin Pumping Engines	

Three Models

Standard $10.00, Junior $5.00, Midget $2.50.
Standard model can be supplied with Lincoln-Highway emblem.

THE MOTO-METER COMPANY, Inc.
148 West 52nd Street   -   -   New York City

California

Route North and West of Lake Tahoe (Direct Route)
For optional route via Carson City East
and South of Tahoe, see page 155

LINCOLN HIGHWAY STATE CONSUL, JOS. E. CAINE,
Oakland, Cal.

GENERAL INFORMATION

C ALIFORNIA, the "Land of Sunshine and Flowers," is rightly named "The Playground of America." He who once comes within its influence usually returns, and often remains in permanent and willing fascination. Climate, that will-o'-the-wisp that has led travelers in search of comfort or health a weary chase over many lands, comes closest to the ideal in California.

California has a coast line of twelve hundred miles. Between the sea and the mountain range, which forms its eastern boundary, lies a fair land of valleys and hills with much variety of products and climate, yet with a strangely unified and equable temperature. For the sight-seer it boasts of Yosemite Valley, one of the most wonderful and beautiful spots in all the world; Lake Tahoe, on the Lincoln Highway, noted for its marvelous coloring in both the water and the surrounding pine-clad mountains, and for the motorist its splendid system of State Highways. Within the year 1916 the State Highway Commission will have completed two 1100-mile boulevards the entire length of the State—one known as the Pacific Highway which will extend through the Sacramento and San Joaquin Valleys from the Oregon to the Mexico line, and the other along the entire Coast, which without a doubt will be the most scenic trip in all America, having a combination of ocean, mountains and the wonderful California Redwood forests.

The tourist will find the Lincoln Highway one of the many beautiful drives in this state. The entire length of the Lincoln Highway from Truckee to Oakland is a state highway, and kept up by the state. About $200,000.00 will be spent on the roads in Placer County alone during 1916. All of the Lincoln Highway in California is in good condition—the major portion of it of concrete. The tourist will be able to make extended drives from Oakland or San Francisco at the western end of the route, either north or south, over excellent roads.

TRUCKEE

N.Y. **S.F.** Pop. 1,600. Alt. 5,280 feet. Nevada County.
3096 **235** Four hotels, 3 garages. Route marked through town and county, signs at town limits. Two railroads, 42 general business places, 1 express company, 1 telegraph company, **5** 1 newspaper, 2 public schools, electric lights, water works.

California

Commercial Club. Truckee has the only Ice Palace in the State of California. Truckee is the scene of the death of the Historic Donner Party who started across the plains in the early 50's and reached Donner Lake (named after the party) when they were snow bound. All but three died of starvation. The roads throughout Nevada County are in excellent condition. Continuous state highway from Truckee to Oakland via Colfax and Auburn.

The easiest way to reach the famous Lake Tahoe from the Lincoln Highway at present, is from Truckee; a ride of but 15 miles up the Truckee River—a beautiful river, over a good road. The scenery is fine on this route as well as over the Sierra Nevada Range, and at the Lake will be found excellent hotel accommodations and good fishing.

TUNNEL UNDER THE RAILROAD.

JUST after crossing under the Central Pacific Railroad, the tourist should walk back to the top of the tunnel, where a fine view of Donner Lake and the distant mountain ranges of Nevada may be had.

After leaving the "Summit," the road follows the Yuba River, a beautiful stream with plenty of trout in its waters.

THE CROSS OF THE DONNER TRAGEDY.

ON the left of the road, but a little way inside the fence, stands the huge wooden cross which marks the spot where the Donner party made their last camp amid whirling snow-flakes in the sudden storm which blocked further progress. Right here they were entrapped for many months until, after what seemed to them, ages of starvation and mental agony, most of them starved, a miserable death, buried in their damp and dismal shelters from ten to twenty feet beneath the snow and ice; the only light coming through the stairway holes which they had cut down through the snow while they yet had the strength.

Near here is the stump of a tree about twenty feet high. The men stood on the snow to chop down this tree.

Standing by the cross in the glorious sunshine of a summer day, it is impossible to realize what it must have meant to those immigrants, after so many months of exhausting travel through desert and plain, to gaze at the tremendous barrier before them, already half hidden in the approaching storm, and to know, that if they could only cross this last mountain range, the fertile valleys of California lay but a short distance beyond.

DONNER

N.Y. S.F. Pop. 50. Placer County.

3101 230 Two hotels. Route marked through village and county.
25 One railroad, 1 general business place, 1 express company, telegraph. Good camping and fishing. Unsurpassed scenery.

California

DONNER LAKE, CALIF.

On the left of the highway is that charming bit of blue water known as Donner Lake, set down in the heart of the Sierras and surrounded by the green forest and immense walls of granite rocks rising to great heights and forming the eastern side of the barrier, the summit of which, even in summer, is covered with snow.

Leave the car and walk down to the shore of this beautiful lake and observe the wonderful scene.

Here is where the advance party of the Donner expedition arrived in time to hastily erect cabins for their protection against the coming storm, which could be plainly seen gathering in the mountains across the lake.

They met the same tragic fate as the Donner family, ten miles back, who did not even have time to erect cabins. Donner, being the captain of the expedition, had hung back to help and guide the stragglers, and so had arrived last.

Several attempts were made by the more hardy spirits of the party to escape over the mountains on foot before the snow became too deep; but when not more than half way to the summit, they were forced in despair to turn back—the snow having already com pletely obliterated the trail and made further progress impossible.

A more beautiful locality can hardly be imagined than this on the shore of Donner Lake, and the tourist feels well repaid for all the possible hardships of the desert when he finally camps in this restful spot.

EMIGRANT GAP

N.Y. **S.F.** Pop. 150. Alt. 5,221 feet. Placer County.

3126 **205** No tourist accommodations. Railroad station, express company, telegraph.

13 Just after crossing the railroad at this place, walk a few feet to the north and there you will find a fine view of Bear Valley. You will be astonished to see such a valley in such a place. Just below, at the foot of the hill, is the big ditch of the Pacific Gas and Electric Company, leading from Lake Spaulding—a reservoir which has one of the highest dams in the world—which furnishes water for irrigation of the fruit lands below, and the distant cities of Sacramento, Oakland and San Francisco.

DUTCH FLAT OR ALTA

N.Y. **S.F.** Pop. 50, Alt. 3,607 feet. Placer County.

3139 **192** Railroad station, telegraph.

4 From the Highway at this point, may be seen the great banks of gravel where the hydraulic mines were operated in the early days of California. There are several large "drift mines" still in operation here.

GOLD RUN

N.Y. **S.F.** Railroad station, telegraph office.

3143 **188**

10

California

COLFAX

N.Y. **S.F.**
3153 **178**

5

Pop. 1,500. Alt. 2,321 feet. Placer County, situated on the west slope of the Sierras. A railroad junction point. Four hotels, 2 garages. Local speed limit 15 miles per hour, enforced. Route marked through town and county, signs at town limits. One railroad crossing at grade, protected. One bank, 2 railroads, 4 general business places, 1 express company, 1 telegraph company, 1 newspaper, electric lights, water works. Rich mining country. L. H. Local Consul, John A. Newman.

WYMAR

N.Y. **S.F.**
3158 **173**

3

Railroad station only.

APPLEGATE

N.Y. **S.F.**
3161 **170**

9

Pop. 65. Placer County. Three hotels. Route marked through village and county. One railroad, 1 express company, 1 telephone company.

AUBURN

N.Y. **S.F.**
3170 **161**

5

Pop. 2,700. Alt. 1,359 feet. County seat, Placer County. Two hotels, 3 garages. Local speed limit 15 miles per hour, enforced. Route marked through town and county. Two banks, 2 railroads, 38 general business places, 1 express company, 1 telegraph company, 2 newspapers, 2 public schools, electric lights, water works. Commercial Club. L. H. Local Consul, J. A. Livingston.

NEW CASTLE

N.Y. **S.F.**
3175 **156**

3

Pop. 500. Gas and oil. Railroad and telegraph station.

PENRYN

N.Y. **S.F.**
3178 **153**

2

Pop. 400. Gas and oil. Railroad station and telegraph.

LOOMIS

N.Y. **S.F.**
3180 **151**

3

Pop. 1,000. Placer County. One hotel, 1 garage. Route marked through town and county, signs at town limits. One bank, 1 railroad, 13 general business places, 1 express company, 1 telegraph company, 1 newspaper, 1 public school, electric lights, water works. Commercial Club. The town is surrounded by orchards of all kinds of fruits, including many orange groves. L. H. Local Consul, G. F. Rowell.

California

ROCKLIN

N.Y. **S.F.** Pop. 1,026. Alt. 247 feet. Placer County.

3183 **148** One railroad, 1 express company, 1 telegraph company. Rocklin has large granite quarries.

4

ROSEVILLE

N.Y. **S.F.** Pop. 2,609. Alt. 200 feet. Placer County.

3187 **144** Four hotels, 2 garages. Local speed limit 15 miles per hour, enforced. Route marked through town and county. One railroad, 1 express company, 1 telephone company.

17 Surrounded by a variety of industrial and scenic wonders. About 8 miles north lies Lincoln, the center of the pottery industry, with the largest pottery works in the west. Large fruit packing operations.

SACRAMENTO

(North and West of Tahoe) Pop. 75,000. Alt. 40 feet. County seat, Sacramento County. Capital of California.

N.Y. **S.F.** Forty-five hotels, 25 garages. Local speed limit 15 miles per hour, enforced. Route marked through city and county. Five railroad crossings at grade, not protected. Ten banks, 3 railroads, 5 interurban roads, 2 express companies, 2 telegraph companies, 3 daily newspapers and several weeklies, 22 public schools. Commercial Club.

3204 **127**

Sacramento is the junction point of the two routes around Lake Tahoe, the route dividing at Reno, Nevada. The tourist by way of Carson City and Placerville (East and South of Tahoe) travels 27 miles farther in reaching this point than has the tourist via Truckee and Auburn (North and West of Tahoe).

13

Mount Lassen, the only live volcano in the United States, is located near Sacramento. Some of the chief points of interest are the Capitol Building, which stands in an unequalled park of thirty-four acres; Fort Sutter, which was established in 1839 by General John A. Sutter, the founder of Sacramento City; the orange and other citrus-fruit orchards near the city; the swimming baths; Chinatown and Japanese quarters. The main system shops of

(East and South of Tahoe) the Southern Pacific and Western Pacific Railroads are located here, also a $2,000,000 packing plant. L. H. Local Consul, L. S. Upson.

N.Y. **S.F.** Here the tourist may connect with the fine system of California roads running north along the coast to Portland, Seattle and British Columbia.

3231 **127**

Sacramento is situated on the east bank of the Sacramento River, just below its confluence with the American River.

Steamers ply from here, down the river, to San Francisco and both sides of the river exhibit scenes of agricultural beauty.

The American Flag was raised over this fort on July 11, 1846.

ELK GROVE

N.Y. **S.F.** Pop. 500. Alt. 51 feet. Sacramento County.

3217 **114** No tourist accommodations. Railroad station, express company, telegraph.

5

California

MC CONNELL

N.Y. **S.F.** Sacramento County.

3222 **109** No tourist accommodations. Railroad station, telegraph.

2

ARNO

N.Y. **S.F.** Pop. 100. Sacramento County.

3224 **107** Meals, garage, gas. Route marked through village and county, signs at approach of village. One railroad, 1 general business place, 1 express company, 1 telegraph company, telephone, 1 public school.

6

GALT

N.Y. **S.F.** Pop. 985. Alt. 47 feet. Sacramento County.

3230 **101** Three hotels, 2 garages. Route marked through town and county. One railroad, 1 express company, 1 telegraph company. The longest iron bridge in California, 1 mile south of Galt. Large fruit orchards. •

8

WOODBRIDGE

N.Y. **S.F.** Pop. 228. San Joaquin County. On the Mokelumne River.

3238 **93** No tourist accommodations. Railroad station, telegraph, express company.

14

California

STOCKTON

N.Y. 3252 **S.F.** 79

Pop. 41,000. Alt. 25 feet. County seat, San Joaquin County, at the head of navigation on the San Joaquin River.

5

Sixteen hotels, 22 garages. Local speed limit 20 miles per hour, enforced. Route marked through city and county, signs at city limits. One railroad crossing at grade, unprotected. Seven banks, 3 railroads, 3 express companies, 2 telegraph companies, 3 daily newspapers. Automobile Club, Commercial Club. Stockton has the greatest flour mills and machinery factories on the coast. L. H. Local Consul, Charles E. Manthey.

FRENCH CAMP

N.Y. 3257 **S.F.** 74

Pop. 350. San Joaquin County.

11 ·

One hotel, 1 garage. Route marked through town and county. Two railroad crossings at grade, not protected. Two railroads, 6 general business places, 1 public school, telephone, electric lights. French camp is the center of a rich farming country. Good salmon fishing in the San Joaquin River 2½ miles away, also duck hunting in the river marshes.

BANTA

N.Y. 3268 **S.F.** 63

Pop. 143. Alt. 27 feet. San Joaquin County.

3

State law governs local speed limit, enforced. Route marked through village and county. One railroad, 1 express company. Grain raising country.

TRACY

N.Y. 3271 **S.F.** 60

Pop. 2,000. Alt. 61 feet. San Joaquin County.

13

Three hotels, 3 garages. State law governs speed limit. Route marked through town and county, signs at town limits. Two railroad crossings at grade, not protected. Two banks, 1 railroad, 25 general business places, 1 express company, 1 telegraph company, 1 newspaper, 1 public school, electric lights, water works. Commercial Club. L. H. Local Consul, H. A. Hull.

ALTAMONT

N.Y. 3284 **S.F.** 47

Pop. 80. Alt. 737 feet. Alameda County.

8

One hotel. Local speed limit 25 miles per hour, enforced. Route marked through town and county. Extensive road improvement. Two railroads, 1 general business place, 1 express company, 1 telegraph company, 1 public school, electric lights.

LIVERMORE

N.Y. 3292 **S.F.** 39

Pop. 2,500. Alt. 487 feet. Alameda County.

18

Five hotels, 3 garages. Local speed limit 10-20 miles per hour, enforced. Route marked through town and county, signs at town limits. Seven miles east lies a series of sand-stone caves evidently formed at some time by the constant wash of an immense body of water. L. H. Local Consul, L. M. McDonald.

California

HAYWARD

N.Y. **S.F.** Pap. 3,500. Alameda County.

3310 **21** Four hotels, 3 garages. Local speed limit 20 miles per hour, enforced. Route marked through town and county. Two banks, 2 railroads, 40 general business places, 2 express companies, 1 telegraph company, 2 newspapers, 4 public schools, electric lights, trolley, water works. Commercial Club. The Lincoln Highway runs through the Dublin Canyon at Hayward. It is one of the main passes through the Coast Range Mountains. Hayward is the center of one of the most beautiful fruit producing sections of California. L. H. Local Consul, H. R. Robinson.

15

OAKLAND

N.Y. **S.F.** Pop. 215,000. Alt. 11 feet. County seat, Alameda County.

3325 **6** Situated on the east shore of San Francisco Bay. It has a healthy and pleasant climate. Seven hotels, 3 express companies, 2 telegraph companies. Large steam ferry boats ply between Oakland and San Francisco. Oakland owns and controls the waterfront, to which much of the word's commerce is brought. Terminus Southern Pacific, Atchison, Topeka & Santa Fe and Western Pacific Railways. Seat of Pacific Theological Seminary (Congregational), Mills College for Girls and various other collegiate institutions. Numerous magnificent mansions. Among its manufacturing and constructive industries are extensive iron works, foundries and machine shops, smelting and metallurgical works, canneries, cotton, flouring and planing mills, tanneries, manufactures of electric cables, etc.

6 L. H. State Consul, Jos. E. Caine, secretary of Commercial Club.

Oakland may be called the "hub" of the automobile roads of California for the beautiful drives radiate in all directions from this city. This is the distributing point for the three great agricultural valleys of the state—the Sacramento, San Joaquin and Santa Clara.

It is but a short run to Berkeley, where the famous Greek Theatre of the University of California is located and the Mission of San Jose is also within easy reach of the motorist.

Oakland is the mainland end of the Lincoln Highway, and a ferry boat may be taken from here across the bay to San Francisco, just six miles away.

Many routes present themselves over roads of varying degrees of excellence Yosemite Park is but one of the many points which will attract the tourist.

SAN FRANCISCO

(North and West of Tahoe) Pop. 525,000. Alt. 9 feet. County seat, San Francisco County. The metropolis of the Pacific coast and the largest and most important city of the region west of the Missouri River. It is built on a peninsula and extends

N.Y. **S.F.** to the Pacific Ocean on the west, the Golden Gate on the

3331 **0** north and San Francisco Bay on the east. It is centrally located on the coast line and has a harbor about seventy miles long and ten miles wide. The narrow but deep entrance to this harbor is known the world over as the

California

(East and
South of
Tahoe)

N.Y.   S.F.
3358   0

"Golden Gate." Its site is largely hilly, and it presents a picturesque appearance from the harbor. Semi-tropical plants flourish in the open air throughout the winter. To the right as the ferry boat crosses the bay is "Goat Island," and toward the Golden Gate is Alcatraz Island, on which is located the United States prison. To cross the bay takes thirty minutes. In 1835 the town of Yerba Buena was settled, and later expanded and annexed the "Mission" and "Presidio" earlier settlements. The settlement was incorporated and the name changed to San Francisco in 1847. San Francisco has many points of interest. Golden Gate Park, consisting of 1,000 acres, affords much interest and amusement. There are many resorts on the beach, among which are the Cliff House, overlooking the famous Seal Rocks, Sutro Heights and Baths. Chinatown is also one of the unique sights offered to tourists. The Presidio and Government Reserve to the north of the Exposition grounds are well worth attention. Local Consul, D. E. Watkins, Secy. California State Automobile Association.

Route East and South of Lake Tahoe
(Via Carson City)
Nevada

RENO

N.Y.	S.F.	(North and West of Tahoe	N.Y.	S.F.
3061	297		3061	270

10

STEAMBOAT SPRINGS

N.Y.	S.F.
3071	287

5

Pop. 23. Alt. 4,613 feet. Washoe County. Railroad station, hotel, camp site, telephone. A few miles east of this point is the famous Comstock lode near Virginia City which produced $700,000,000 in gold and silver in less than ten years. Has 700 miles of underground workings.

WASHOE

N.Y.	S.F.
3076	282

5

Pop. 29. Alt. 5,032 feet. Washoe County. Railroad station, drinking water, radiator water, camp site, telephone.

FRANKTOWN

N.Y.	S.F.
3081	277

12

Pop. 400. Alt. 5,054 feet. Washoe County. Railroad station, telegraph, drinking water, radiator water.

CARSON CITY

N.Y.	S.F.
3093	265

15

Pop. 3,000. Alt. 4,706 feet. County seat, Ormsby County and capital of the State of Nevada. Four hotels, 4 garages. Local speed limit 15 miles per hour, enforced. Route marked through town and county; signs at town limits. One bank, 1 railroad, 85 general business places, 1 express company, 1 telegraph company, 3 newspapers, 1 public school, electric lights, waterworks. Near the city are the state penitentiary, the convict operated prison farm, the Stewart Indian School, and the State Orphan's Home. It will repay the tourist to detour to the famous mining camp of Virginia City, only a few miles distant. Local Consuls, Geo. M. Anderson, W. J. Maxwell. County Consul, L. F. Adamson.

(Route East and South of Lake Tahoe)

Nevada

GLENBROOK
N.Y. **S.F.** Alt. 4,453 feet. Douglas County.
3108 **250** Hotel, meals, lodging, gas, oil, camp site, telephone.

3

CAVE ROCK
N.Y. **S.F.** Douglas County.
3111 **247** No tourist accommodations. Only a landmark.

7

EDGEWOOD
N.Y. **S.F.** Pop. 227. Alt. 2,953 feet. Eldorado County.
3118 **240** No tourist accommodations. Railroad station.

1

LAKESIDE PARK
N.Y. **S.F.** Note: Here proceed direct to Meyers on the L. H. (8 mi.)
3119 **239** or detour west to Al Tahoe (beautiful summer resort)
short drive, and to Tallac, thence on to Meyers (on Lincoln Highway) and continue to Placerville. Or the tourist
8 can follow a good road from Tallac along the west shore
of the lake to Truckee and thence west on the L. H. (north
of the lake route) to Auburn. Lakeside Park is on the
Nevada-Calfornia State line.

Route East and South of Lake Tahoe
California

MEYERS
N.Y. **S.F.** Alt. 3,759 feet. Eldorado County.
3127 **231** No tourist accommodations.

3

SIERRA NEVADA SUMMIT
N.Y. **S.F.** Alt. 7,394 feet. Eldorado County.
3130 **228** No tourist accommodations.

3

PHILLIPS
N.Y. **S.F.** Alt. 6,871 feet. Eldorado County.
3133 **225** No tourist accommodations.

4

(Route East and South of Lake Tahoe)

California

STRAWBERRY
N.Y. **S.F.** Alt. 5,695 feet. Eldorado County.
3137 **221** No tourist accommodations.

10

KYBURZ
N.Y. **S.F.** Eldorado County.
3147 **211** No tourist accommodations.

10

RIVERTON
N.Y. **S.F.** Eldorado County.
3157 **201** No tourist accommodations.

11

SPORTMAN'S HALL
N.Y. **S.F.** Eldorado County.
3168 **190** No tourist accommodations.

4

CAMINO
N.Y. **S.F.** Pop. 100. Eldorado County.
3172 **186** No tourist accommodations. Railroad station, telegraph.

7

PLACERVILLE
N.Y. **S.F.** Pop. 3,000. Alt. 1,875 feet. County seat Eldorado County.
3179 **179** Four hotels, 4 garages. Local speed limit 10 miles per hour, enforced. Route marked through town and county. Extensive road improvement. One railroad crossing at grade, not protected. One bank, 2 railroads, 43 general business places, 1 express company, 1 telegraph company, 2 newspapers, 3 public schools, electric lights, water works. Commercial Club. Sutters Fort and Monument at Coloma, 8 miles from Placerville, commemorating and marking the spot where gold was discovered in California in 1848, is well worth the detour. L. H. Local Consul, Dr. O. P. Fitch.

7

ELDORADO]
N.Y. **S.F.** Population 100. Eldorado County.
3186 **172** Gas and oil. No tourist accommodations. Route marked through county.

5

(Route East and South of Lake Tahoe)

California

SHINGLE SPRINGS
N.Y. **S.F.** Population 50. No tourist accommodations. Telegraph
3191 **167** station.

8

CLARKSVILLE
N.Y. **S.F.** Railroad stop. No tourist accommodations.
3199 **159**

3

WHITE ROCK
N.Y. **S.F.** No tourist accommodations. Telegraph station.
3202 **156**

7

FOLSOM
N.Y. **S.F.** Pop. 1,500. Alt. 180 feet. Sacramento County.
3209 **149** Two hotels, 2 garages. Route marked through town and
county; signs at town limits. One railroad crossing at
grade, unprotected. One bank, 1 railroad, 12 general business places, 1 express company, 1 telegraph company, 1
newspaper, 2 public schools, electric lights, water works.
2 The State Penitentiary is located here. This point is one
of interest on account of its pioneer history during the
"gold rush" of the late '40's. Fruit, grains, vegetables
and mining are its resources. The scenery is varied and
beautiful.

NATOMA
N.Y. **S.F.** Pop. 150. Sacramento County.
3211 **147** No tourist accommodations, merely a mining camp. One
railroad.

8

MILLS
N.Y. **S.F.** Sacramento County.
3219 **139** No tourist accommodations. Railroad station, telegraph,
express.

3

MAYHEW
N.Y. **S.F.** Pop. 90. Alt. 57 feet. Sacramento County.
3222 **136** Railroad station, telegraph.

1

(Route East and South of Lake Tahoe)

California

MANLOVE

N.Y.	S.F.	Sacramento County.
3223	135	No tourist accommodations. Railroad station, telegraph.

2

PERKINS

N.Y.	S.F.	Pop. 250. Alt. 50 feet. Sacramento County.
3225	133	No tourist accommodations. Railroad station, telegraph, express.

6

SACRAMENTO

N.Y.	S.F.	(North and West of Tahoe)	N.Y.	S.F.
3231	127		3204	127

Seeing America First

THE Lincoln Highway is the direct arterial line of motor travel from which practically all points of scenic or historic interest in the United States may be conveniently reached. All of the national parks, including Yellowstone, Glacier, Yosemite and Grand Canyon, can be reached more or less conveniently, and over roads that may in the main be considered travelable.

The two states of New Mexico and Arizona are replete with interest, both historic and scenic. Much road improvement has been begun and is now being prosecuted in these two states.

These roads lead to the Grand Canyon of the Colorado, the Needles, Roosevelt Dam, Santa Fe, Petrified Forest, Salton Sea, and innumerable points worthy of study and observation.

From the Lincoln Highway this section of the United States is best reached by either one of two roads:

First—It is suggested that you leave the Lincoln Highway at Cheyenne, proceed south through Denver, Colorado Springs and Pueblo, striking the Santa Fe Trail at Trinidad, and on through to Sante Fe, Albuquerque, Carthage, Springerville, Holbrook, Flagstaff, Kingman, the Needles, etc. The Roosevelt Dam, located between Springerville and Phoenix, is best reached by a road via the former point; or

Second—If you have journeyed over the Lincoln Highway to the Pacific coast and desire to return east via this most attractive southern route, it is suggested that you take the Pacific coast road from San Francisco to Los Angeles, thence on to San Diego and the Santa Fe Trail, reaching the same points as have been previously enumerated. You can then proceed north to Colorado Springs and the Lincoln Highway, connecting at Cheyenne. You can well spend a month in making this detour, and seeing the wonders which are offered. Weeks alone might be spent in a study of the prehistoric cliff-dwellers excavations which are proceeding under government supervision and which are also being prosecuted by the various educational institutions of the country.

Considering the vast distances and areas and the small population no section of the United States today is seeing such improvement in its highways as these Southwestern States.

Index

Index—(Continued)

Index—(Continued)

Index—(Continued)

Index—(Continued)

Advertiser's Index

Advertiser's Index—(Continued)

Advertiser's Index—(Continued)

March 27, 1918. For 6 the machine out
& new ... Batley ... 16.

CPSIA information can be obtained
at www.ICGtesting.com
Printed in the USA
LVOW13s1300020518
575695LV00011B/269/P

9 781376 284799